Praise for One Woman in the Himalayas

"You will love trekking with Tracy along Nepal's remote Annapurna Circuit as she faces obstacles and challenges that test her grit, while also weaving in the fascinating culture of the Nepalese people and the joys of Type II fun."

Kit Parks, Host,
Active Travel Adventures
and Adventure Travel Show podcasts

"This book is part Nepal travelogue, part inspiration, and part universal life lessons—all shared with heart and soul."

Janet Hanpeter,
Chief Travel Adventurer, Planet Janet Travels

'Tracy Pawelski has done it again—disrupted her comfort zone to take a risk on herself. This time she's trekking in the Himalayas. When things go awry, will wits and stamina be enough to get her back on track? This true story is a literal 'cliff-hanger."

Stacey Wittig, author,
Spiritual and Walking Guide: León to Santiago

D1329879

"From one of the most remote places on earth Tracy propels readers to embrace our courage and common humanity and apply it to our own families and communities. This book is a must-read for all women, whether they're considering a Himalayan hike or looking for inspiration and introspection as they face major life choices."

Nell McCormack Abom, President,
Nell McCormack Abom Communications

"The joy of Tracy's journey is her willingness to peel away the veneer from the confidence that an American woman—careerist, wife, mother—must project in a world where the survivors are the winners. Even when the trek doesn't go as planned, we meet her adapting and crafting a journey of discovery—discovery of a world of wondrous beauty and inner strength."

M. Diane McCormick, author,
Well-Behaved Taverns Seldom Make History:
Pennsylvania Pubs Where Rabble-Rousers and Rum
Runners Stirred Up Revolutions

ONE WOMAN IN THE HIMALAYAS

Not Every Idea is a Good Idea,
But You Don't Know Until You Try

Tracy Pawelski

ONE WOMAN IN THE HIMALAYAS

NOT EVERY IDEA IS A GOOD IDEA, BUT YOU DON'T KNOW UNTIL YOU TRY

To contact Tracy:

Website .... www.tracypawelski.com
LinkedIn .... www.linkedin.com/in/tracypawelski
Email .... tracy.pawelski63@gmail.com
Facebook .... One Woman's Camino
Instagram .... tracypawelski

David Whyte's poem, *The Faces at Braga*, from Where Many Rivers Meet, is printed with permission from ©Many Rivers Press, Langley, WA USA.

To contact the publisher, Gravitas Press, visit https://GravitasPress.com

Printed in the United States of America

ISBN 978-1-7359435-1-0

Book Strategist & Editor ..... Bonnie Budzowski
Cover Design .... Bobbie Fox Fratangelo

Dedication

This story is dedicated to Chuck who lit the fire and Ram who led the way.

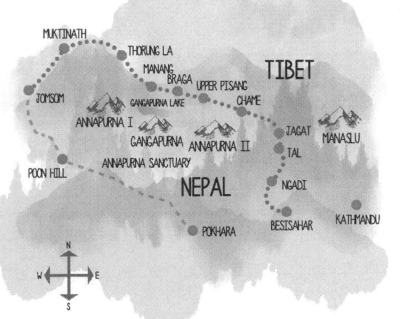

CONTENTS

--------- Chapter 1 ---------

THE ALLURE OF ADVENTURE

"How on earth did I get here?" I pant under my breath—feeling as if I have no breath left.

I am sucking for air high in the Himalayas, climbing in altitude and moving in the direction of Manang, an ancient trading village in Nepal. I coax my body onward. One foot. Next foot. Repeat.

The blood thumping in my ears is keeping the beat. One foot. Next foot. Repeat. Sweat under my arms and hat makes me feel damp and clammy. As I think about my bucket of hot water several days ago in the village of Pisang, I fear I have set a new personal low for cleanliness.

Up ahead, my guide leads the way, while my porter lags behind. We have been hiking for more than a week in the shadow of the world's highest mountain during which time I have struggled with a series of changed plans and decisions made in thin air.

Manang is my turn-around point on the Annapurna Circuit, considered one of the best treks in the world. Shaped like a horseshoe, the full circuit travels 130 miles around the Annapurna massif and takes about three weeks to walk. This busy pilgrimage and trading route typically begins in the Marsyangdi River Valley and climbs past subtropical rice terraces, through forests thick with rhododendron, and into the thin air of Thorung La, one of the highest mountain passes in the world. A cultural mash-up, the route connects the Hindu lowlands with the Buddhist highlands as it skirts along the Tibetan border, a virtual no-man's-land between China and Nepal. All the while, the trek offers views of the highest peaks on earth.

But how did I get here in the first place? A domino of decisions had turned my world upside-down. Decisions all of my own making.

The first decision—which I made with the full support of my husband, Rick—was to leave my corporate gig as the U.S. spokesperson for a large international company. I had been looking for the right moment to step away from a stressful corporate career after more than three decades of professional success. Now that I was in my 50s, I was ready to pivot. In fact, I was in the terrifying thick of it—at a turning point that required me to decide which way to go next. As I looked out on the horizon, I couldn't see too far, but I fixed my sight on our daughter, Juliet, and her plans to walk 500 miles across Spain on

El Camino de Santiago. I asked for permission—could I come along? —and remarkably, Juliet said yes.

My second decision—to walk on El Camino de Santiago—offered me an opportunity to think about what I needed to learn and where I wanted to go next. Before leaving for the Camino, I did my research; I knew that this was a spiritual journey and a calling for many pilgrims who traveled its path. For a thousand years, believers had sacrificed and suffered their way to Santiago de Compostela to pay tribute to the Apostle St. James. I didn't go on El Camino de Santiago with a believer's need for soul-searching and absolution. I didn't go looking for transformation. But that's what happened. I wrote about this journey in my book, *One Woman's Camino*.

When I returned from Spain, I was hooked on the experience of long-distance walking, and I had this crazy idea to keep going. After all, you don't figure everything out in 35 days, and I wanted to continue to look for answers and adventure. Three months later, I was headed to Nepal as part of a small expedition led by an Irish friend named Chuck. Decision number three.

On the Camino, people from all over the world find themselves connecting with each other and bonding like families. The experience puts pilgrims on a common path, living a modest lifestyle, and walking together through all kinds of conditions. The intensity of this shared journey accelerates the time it takes to form deep and lasting friendships. Early on, our group formed a three-generation family that included Juliet and me from America, our Dutch friend, Caroline, and Chuck and John from Ireland.

Chuck was one of my favorite people from El Camino, a big-hearted Irishman who could fill a book with colorful stories. Is every Irishman a natural storyteller? The Irish gift of gab compels you to take a seat and get comfortable.

Chuck was the oldest member of our Camino family, a husband, father, and grandfather. At 70 years young, he regularly hiked the craggy coastline of Ireland and occasionally scaled the high peaks of Scotland. Chuck was arranging a return trip to Nepal, using his time on the Camino to train and prepare. He was working with an in-country guide to make his plans.

"Tom Paine, a true hero of mine, held that life has to be a daring adventure or nothing at all," Chuck mused as we walked.

We talked about enjoying the thrill of new places and, in Chuck's words, "looking for the unexpected, opting for the road less traveled." Ours was an easy friendship forged as we walked and talked our way across Spain, describing our lives back home, our interest in different cultures, and love of big mountains.

"I've always loved the mountains," he told me. "Their sheer size is not only a reminder of our own scale, but also our place alongside them. It's in the mountains that I feel a connection. We are as much a part of them as they are of us.

"So, I've decided to mark my 70th birthday with a 'last swing of the gate' experience by tackling the Annapurna Circuit and its Thorung La pass at 18,000 feet."

Chuck's talk of Nepal fascinated me. I was jumping at the chance to experience the majesty of the high Himalayas. Who wouldn't want to trek along an ancient trading route, sharing the path with yak herders and Sherpas? The Himalayas are home to eight of the world's ten highest mountains. I'd been told that they are awe-inspiring and intimidating, a place to feel both big and small at the same time.

When Chuck suggested that I join his trek to Nepal, the call of adventure was ringing loudly in my ears.

The trip would mean once again setting off for an extended period without Rick. Unlike my walk across Spain, I would be without my daughter as well. When I asked Rick what he thought of the idea, from his always-generous wellspring of support, he said, "I think you should go to Nepal!"

Rick shares the draw that adventure has on me. He likes to say that "beaten paths are for beaten men." So, when I had decided to walk across Spain with Juliet in order to reset my course, Rick was in my corner. My Camino with Juliet was such a gift that it seemed like I should keep walking, keep searching, keep exploring. After all, I was still in a state of transition and finding my way.

Just six months earlier, I had been in a corporate boardroom, more concerned about reputation management and crisis communications than the risk of hypothermia in the Himalayas. I realize that most people have neither the opportunity nor the appetite to head to the other side of the globe to test their mettle. So why did I say yes to the Annapurna Circuit? Why did it become something I increasingly needed to do?

My answer at the time seemed simple. "If not now, then when?"

I've always been a sure-footed decision-maker, not intimidated by navigating the turbulent waters of uncertainty. I've made mistakes along the way, for sure. But my personal pattern is to trust my gut and go for it. I have enough faith to know I'll land on my feet. Chalk it up to a generous heap of chutzpah well beyond the typical single serving.

Walking the Annapurna Circuit had not been a lifelong goal of mine; in fact, I really didn't know much about it. Visiting Nepal had not been on my bucket list, even though I am naturally drawn to new places. I said to myself, "Hmm, Nepal. I've never been there. Perhaps I will find what I'm looking for among the world's tallest peaks."

And so, the seed of interest was planted, and my determination to hike the Annapurna Circuit began to grow.

When I said I would go to Nepal, I was pretty excited to build on the success of my walk across Spain. After all, I was in the best shape of my life. Why not step a little further into the unknown? But as I learned more about this journey, my palms got sweaty and my stomach started to flip. After I had made the decision, my adrenaline started to spike. Regularly. My amygdala flew into action; that's the crazy little part of the brain that sniffs out fear and has been keeping us alive for thousands of years. It felt like my heart rate was constantly racing. Did I really know what I was getting into?

I had made my decision, perhaps not recklessly, but certainly impulsively, and now I was trying to come to terms with it. Red flags started to appear. The more diligent I became with my research, the more I learned about unpredictable weather, trekkers dying of exposure, and an inadequate infrastructure in a fragile part of the world. I said yes and then began a painful journey into second-guessing my decision. Little did I know at that time how often on this journey I would have to stop and ask myself, "How badly do you want this, Tracy? Will you keep going or will you turn back?"

This is a story about what happens when your decisions don't turn out as you planned. Because, of

course, they never do. If you pay attention to the
subtitle of this book—not every idea is a good idea,
but you don't know until you try—you might think
that my trek to Nepal was a bad move, even a regret-
table one. It's true that I may not have adequately
weighed all of the risks beforehand, but I went
anyway.

In my view, women are naturally gifted decision-
makers with abundant experience thinking on our feet.
We make thousands of snap decisions throughout
each day to keep our lives and the lives of our loved
ones glued together. There are myriad mundane
decisions: What should I wear for the big pitch?
Should I call Mom now or later? Yoga or cardio?
These decisions punctuate our days and keep the
never-ending to-do list moving forward. Most are
made in a split second. No second guessing. No
gnashing of teeth. Well, except for what to wear.

And then there are decisions that carry more
weight, like the medical, legal, and financial decisions
we make at work, and those we make for ourselves,
our aging parents, and our children. The way we plot
our careers and follow our dreams.

Making decisions is what we women do: solve
problems and make decisions. But how confident are
we about the game-changers? These are the decisions
that offer the greatest opportunity for personal growth
but can shake us to our core. I didn't know as I
prepared to travel to Nepal how much this journey

would test my limits and how hard I would have to work to keep fear from overwhelming me.

A wise old friend once said, "First you make a decision. Then you make it the right decision." I had made an audacious decision to join the expedition and now I was trying to make it the right decision. Why was this adventure so important to me? There were no guarantees that the weather, the altitude, or any number of unknowns wouldn't present a daunting challenge. Still, I knew I might never have the same opportunity to see this part of the world again, and it isn't like me to pass up a new adventure.

Autumn, when Chuck was planning to make the trip, is the right time to trek in Nepal. The summer monsoon season is typically followed by drier weather and more comfortable temperatures. In spite of the uncertainties involved, the plan made sense to me. So, I laid out my hiking gear and booked my flights to Kathmandu. The allure was irresistible.

---------- Chapter 2 ----------

HOLY CRAP

When my mother got her first passport in the 1960s, it was a combined passport for both her and my dad and included a picture of the two of them. But the U.S. State Department listed only my dad's name on this official document. What would happen at the border if a wife ever traveled without her husband?

Today, in the 21st century, women run for elected office, explore space, build companies, and lead countries. You might argue that we are not on equal footing with our male counterparts, but we certainly have female role models who show us not only what can be done, but also what is being done.

Women think nothing today of traveling alone, moving across the country or even across the world to take a new job. After walking El Camino de Santiago, Juliet moved to Alaska to teach in the Aleutian Islands and eventually to Costa Rica to teach English at a small language school in San Jose. For decades now, we've now been raising girls to believe that they can do anything, which, of course, they can.

Rick and I raised both our kids, Danny and Juliet, to aim high and dream big. When Juliet was teaching in Alaska, our son was also living his best life a long way from home. Danny had chosen to go west for college, leaving a close-knit group of friends in Pennsylvania for an entirely new slice of life at the University of Colorado. He never regretted his decision to step in a different direction, and his trajectory changed as a result.

Personally, I was no stranger to an embrace of risk-taking, whether it was managing my career or seeking increasingly big adventures through travel. But let me be clear; when I talk about taking risks, I am not talking about putting personal safety at risk. Women always have safety on our minds, especially when we tread on new or unfamiliar ground. I am, though, talking about our natural appetite for risk-taking. How ready are we to disrupt the status quo and take a gamble on ourselves?

My appetite for adventure was offset by the fact that I was stepping out of my comfort zone by joining Chuck's trek to Nepal. I figured it was a real privilege to have this opportunity to go to a place I would never visit alone. While I could hear the call of adventure, I certainly didn't want to go it alone.

Chuck and I planned our trip on WhatsApp calls. This app enabled us to make free international calls to discuss what the trip would cost, what we would need to take with us, and what we should expect on the route. On one of the calls, Chuck informed me that the other two people who were lined up to go, a couple of hill-walking friends from Belfast, had pulled out of the trip. The man had broken a rib and wouldn't be ready by October to trek a rigorous route. He asked Chuck to postpone until the following spring, but Chuck had purchased his flights and was determined to go. Chuck told me that, of course, my decision to continue was entirely up to me.

"If you're still going," I said, "I'm in."

I didn't get myself to this point to let a change in the composition of the group change my mind. After all, I didn't know these folks, so their involvement had little impact on my skin in the game. I felt as though I had made a commitment to myself that I was not willing to reconsider. Despite restless nights worrying about whether I had made the right decision to go, I wasn't prepared to exit through the door that had just opened for me. My decision to continue didn't seem like a big one at the time, but it would be the first of many changes that would alter the nature of my experience in Nepal.

We made our arrangements to fly into Kathmandu, Chuck from his home in Belfast and me from the East Coast of the United States. Chuck charted a plan to spend a few days in the capital and then board a flight to Pokhara, a resort town that serves as a jumping off point for the Annapurna Circuit. Our guide, Bhimsen, would meet us in Pokhara, and we'd get started on a thirteen-day trek from Besisahar to Jomsom, after which we would make our way back to Pokhara. I read as much as I could about the circuit, provisioned my pack and started prepping, not unlike the way I had prepared to walk across Spain.

But Nepal is not Spain. There are endless new details to think about. I will be walking from a sub-tropical climate into freezing temperatures and onto snowpack. The items I will need in my pack run the gamut from fast-wicking t-shirts to a down jacket, subzero thermals, and waterproof everything.

I put my pack on my back and walk every day. On the weekends, Rick and I hike the nearby Appalachian Trail, setting a fast pace on the footpaths in the area. Since I live close to sea level, I ask a friend who is a personal trainer for tips on getting my body—and mostly my lungs—ready to handle the altitude. Based on his advice, I try interval training to improve my aerobic capacity and counter the effects of the altitude. Since I am not much of a runner, this type of high-intensity training makes me feel unprepared and inadequate.

My cardio workouts include strenuous walks with a friend who is getting ready for her own expedition to the Asian Kingdom of Bhutan. Kim and I hike with packs on our sweaty backs up to a stone bench where we sit looking across the Cumberland Valley. Picturesque red barns dot the farm fields below us and we pick out our favorite ski hill on the faraway ridge. We talk about how we both love exploring out-of-the-way places and foreign cultures, especially on foot.

I research how to handle my money in Nepal. Money was easy to access in Spain with ATMs located on the corner in every town. I left for Spain with a few hundred euro in my pocket and knew I'd be able to resupply along the way. I can't be so sure about money in Nepal, so I order my Nepalese rupees from the bank. When I pick them up, I am given a given a stack of rupees in denominations of 1,000 and 500. The exchange rate of 100 rupees to one dollar makes my wad of bills so thick, well, it could choke a donkey.

Access to clean water is a big concern in the Himalayas. Good hydration is not just nice to have in this corner of the world but part of survival. In Spain, potable water was available throughout the journey. We could fill our canteens before we left our lodgings each morning and refill them at public pumps along the trail. In the mountains of Nepal, clean drinking water can be hard to find. The risk of exposure to bacteria like *E. coli* or parasites like Giardia require that I take a new level of precaution. I think of everything I can and buy a portable water purifier called a Steripen to zap any bacteria in the water.

I also book an appointment to update my immunizations and carefully review my med kit. I still have ample supplies left over from El Camino to take care of my feet. Experience with my own aches and the pains of walking five to eight hours a day means an abundant supply of ibuprofen, sleep aids and a knee support for my tricky right knee, just in case. I beg my doctor for a regimen of ciprofloxacin, a high-dose antibiotic that I will use only if I need it.

And, of course, I read up on Acute Mountain Sickness (AMS). This is serious stuff, which can affect even the fittest individuals. Many people who find themselves above 10,000 feet experience some degree of discomfort, including head and body aches, sleeplessness, and shortness of breath. At its worst, AMS can result in a high-altitude cerebral edema, a buildup of fluid on the brain that can kill you if you don't get to lower ground fast. I investigate a pre-scription for a high-altitude medication and decide against it. You have to take these meds before you know if you'll need them, and they have ugly side effects such as fatigue and nausea.

It's easy to lose the joy of travel during this period of thinking, rethinking, and planning for the worst. My experience in crisis communications pushes me to prepare for any eventuality. In fact, I am well aware that managing risk is all about preparing for your nightmare scenarios and thinking through every detailed step in response.

People who handle high-stress situations for a living, such as first responders and crisis commun-icators, come in two distinctive shapes and sizes: those who thrive from living on the edge and have ice running through their veins, and those who are skilled but who find crises exhausting and stressful. I fall into the second camp.

I spend this period trying to remind myself why I travel, why I stretch and challenge myself, and why Nepal. As I have done in the past, I find myself waiting. Waiting to walk.

The in-between times are the toughest for me. Too much time to overanalyze. Even elite adventurers—which certainly does not describe me—experience what's called 'anticipatory anguish'—moments prior to an expedition that are filled with self-doubt and second thoughts.

During this process of getting my mind and body ready for my trek in the Himalayas, I realize that the risks I am about to take far surpass anything I faced while walking from town to town across rural Spain. While the Thorung La pass, at 18,000 feet, is not like climbing Mount Everest, the dangers of frostbite, avalanches, and rapid weather changes are real.

And then there is this: a year prior, during the very same week that Chuck and I plan to trek the Annapurna Circuit, forty people died crossing the high pass, victims of a freak blizzard that caught them unexpectedly.

May and October are typically ideal months to trek in the Himalayas. But a late-season cyclone named Hudhud hit northern India the previous October, dropping buckets of rain at lower altitudes. At 18,000 feet in the mountains, that kind of weather added up to big snow. Trekkers were caught completely unprepared for winter whiteout conditions and waist-high—by some accounts, shoulder-deep—snow. Hundreds were stranded; many became disoriented and got lost on the pass as they tried to reach safety. Both guides and trekkers died of exposure.

Rick and I discuss that a late-season cyclone is unlikely to happen again this year, but the thought of it plays big in my mind. I mean, wake-up-in-the-middle-of-the-night, big.

"What are the chances of this happening again?" I ask my actuarial husband, an expert in calculating risk.

"Almost none," he replies, prepared to move on to the next subject. Not the answer that I need.

"Aren't you worried about me?" I demand to know.

"You have always made good decisions. I've seen you handle every situation you've faced. I trust that you will handle whatever comes your way in Nepal as well."

Damn. Just as I am getting ready to blame Rick for not worrying enough about my welfare, I think to myself, "What's a better measure of love: an abundance of trust or an abundance of worry?"

Clearly, I am worried enough for the both of us. No wonder my amygdala is in overdrive. I am traveling to an environment that can and does kill people. My heart races, and I have trouble not fearing the worst. After all, when you are trying to plan for the worst, it's hard not to become consumed by it.

I am no stranger to letting worry sneak up on me. Before I left for El Camino, I was having a love affair with worry. Was my body strong enough to walk 500 miles? Would I love the journey or hate it? Would this long walk bring Juliet and me closer or drive a wedge between us? Had I made the right decision to leave my job when I did?

Women are masterful at the art of worrying. We have perfected this unhelpful character trait and have turned it into an art form. We tuck worry into our purse right next to our lipstick. We unpack it, repack it, and can get consumed by it.

Chuck and I have regular conversations during this time about provisioning and packing. He advises me to buy a bivvy bag just in case we find ourselves in a storm on the pass. Bivvy is shorthand for bivouac, and a bivvy bag is used by mountaineers as a temporary outdoor shelter for high-exposure camping. We would use the bivvy bags if we were caught in a snowstorm without a nearby hut for shelter. The plan would be to dig a snow hole and wait out the storm.

The thought of the bivvy bag sends me over the edge. After all my planning for the worst, this is the scenario I am either unwilling or unable to process. So, I do what any reasonable woman would do; I stop listening and vow that I will take my chances without a bivvy bag. If I need to dig a snow hole to survive, well, I guess I won't.

That doesn't mean I'm not going to Nepal. Once I say that I'm going to do something, I almost always do it, sometimes at my own peril. But I am not going with a bivvy bag. That contingency is one that I am not willing to face.

Chapter 3

NOT WHAT I EXPECTED

Rick and I share a poignant goodbye under the Qatar Airways sign outside of Philadelphia Airport's Terminal A. I wish he were coming along to share the journey, watch the sun rise over the Himalayas, and later look back and laugh about the same stories. Rick reassures me that my trek has an end date just three short weeks away. He says he looks forward to when we have the time to take more grand adventures together.

For now, it is just me taking off.

When Rick and I started dating more than twenty years ago, I was working in the Executive Office of the President and living in Washington, D.C. Rick was just getting his actuarial career started in Baltimore, so we navigated a medium-distance relationship before I took off for Mexico for three months of language classes and cultural immersion. I had already set the wheels into motion for my homestays with Mexican families and wasn't exactly sure where I wanted to live and what I wanted to do at the end of the three months. Our young love was tested by time and distance.

Rick sent me off to Mexico with a cassette tape of songs that he wrote when he was a struggling musician in Nashville. I played that cassette tape until I wore it out. We wrote letters and shared the details of our days as my time in Mexico ticked down. Our courtship was cemented in the pages of long letters, penned from two countries and sealed with yearning.

> *I carry your heart with me (I carry it in my heart) I am never without it*
>
> ~ e.e. cummings

Now Rick hugs me good-bye, which requires a big bear hug to get his arms around two backpacks—a daypack strapped in front and my big pack in the back. Then Rick is gone, back to work and keeping the home fires burning while I begin a journey of nearly 8,000 miles to the other side of the world. Everything I have been planning, training, and working for is now beginning. What may have been abstract for months is suddenly very real.

My Qatar Air flight from Philadelphia to Doha, the capital of Qatar, is a 12-hour slog. Since I can't sleep on planes, I watch six movies on the little screen embedded into the seat in front of me, just staring at the screen to pass the long, boring hours in transit.

I had heard of Qatar but not Doha, a tourism hub and major crossroads of the world. Loudspeakers announce connections from Nigeria, Ethiopia, Iraq, Thailand, India, and Nepal.

The airport is a fascinating place to people-watch, and my long layover provides plenty of time to do it. Passersby are speaking languages that sound quite different from anything I've heard in my travels throughout Europe and South America. I hear clicks and whistles and sounds that are totally unfamiliar to my western ear. Sitting comfortably in what feels like a global on-ramp, women pass by in full burkas and colorful Indian saris; men wear hats, turbans, and headgear that I've never before seen. Everyone is neat, polite, and orderly. As the many nationalities walk by, I feel part of a global community. While we may look or worship differently, there are families all over the world just like mine.

Aboard my final leg, I chat in broken English with the Nepali man who sits beside me. This is my first conversation with anyone since leaving Philadelphia and I am ready for companionship. My new friend explains that he is traveling home to Kathmandu for the big Hindu festival that brings families together once a year just like our Christmas.

"Did you hear about last night's earthquake?" he asks casually.

My eyes grow wide. "Earthquake? Another earthquake?" I ask. "How bad was it?"

The Nepali man doesn't know, and just like that, my rosy, chirpy thoughts of feeling a part of the world disappear. That gnawing fear in the pit of my belly makes me ask myself again, "What in the world have I been thinking?"

Nepal is one of the poorest countries in the world and, therefore, even more vulnerable to natural disasters that regularly destroy roads, schools, and the power grid. If you think about the geology of the region, you can begin to imagine the force that created the highest and most rugged range in the world. No wonder these mountains are considered sacred.

In April of my year to walk the Annapurna Circuit, an earthquake registering 7.8 on the Richter scale devastated the Kathmandu Valley and the area around Everest. A conservative estimate reported that 9,000 people died. Priceless historical sites, such as temples and royal palaces, across the capital of Kathmandu fell into piles of rubble. The earthquake triggered an avalanche on Mount Everest, making April 25, 2015 the deadliest day on the mountain in history.

Tourists from all over the world quickly cancelled their travel plans. Nepal, a country that depends upon foreign dollars, reeled even further in the aftermath of their worst natural disaster in eighty years. And that is saying something in a region commonly beset by earthquakes, landslides, monsoons, and cyclones.

That year, 2015, became a year of destruction. This is not like the Chinese Zodiac Year of the Dragon, the Rabbit, or the Rat, printed with predictions on the placemat at the local Chef Wong's. It was a year of unprecedented damage and death. Concerned about conditions, the number of trekkers decreased by almost half. Before leaving, Chuck and I weren't sure what to expect as a result of the earthquake, especially in the Himalayas. Information coming out of Nepal was spotty. As far as we could tell, the teahouses in the Annapurna region were still standing. These modest, mostly wooden structures along the circuit would serve as our lodgings in the mountains. We knew the circuit was open for trekking, but we didn't have concrete information about the extent of the damage or how services might be limited. This lack of information adds to my uncertainty. Will this trip be worth the risk? I check in with myself and decide that my answer is yes.

Down in the Kathmandu Valley, the rebuilding process is moving at a snail's pace. After an initial groundswell of international support following the quake, the First World has moved on to other priorities, shifting its attention and resources to other parts of the world. UNESCO seems to be one of the few parties working to repair the destruction and providing humanitarian aid to people on the ground.

Some of the slow progress is the result of the political dysfunction in Nepal that leaves the country deeply divided and without strong and stable leadership. In that vacuum, Nepal is an easy pawn in the hands of its more powerful neighbors. The Indian government treats Nepal like a client-state and applies political pressure for its own ends. China is building roads and investing in hydroelectric dams, but Nepal always seems to pay a high price in return. Nepal's natural resources, particularly its cheap labor and unlimited supply of fresh water, make it an easy target.

Nepali men refer to the only work available to them as the 3Ds—dangerous, dirty, and difficult. When it comes to being in the middle of the India and China power play, Nepal and its people always draw the short straw.

As a gesture of our shared future on this planet, Chuck and I decide to use our trek to raise awareness and funds to help Nepali children get back to school following the earthquake. Since so many schools were destroyed, Chuck sets up a fundraising website to help build temporary schools for the kids. Funds are channeled through a UK-based charity that works with local partners to improve education, health, and living conditions throughout Nepal. By contributing to just one temporary school, Chuck and I hope to help in a small way.

Despite daunting odds and difficult conditions, I will discover that the heart-warming, positive spirit of the Nepalese people is what you see first and what you remember last. The Hindus and Buddhists of Nepal have co-existed in relative harmony throughout the centuries. Everywhere we go we will meet Nepalese people who are eager to welcome us to their country. I marvel at their resilience, good nature, and heart.

* * * * *

When I land in Kathmandu and am back in Wi-Fi range in the airport, my phone buzzes with several WhatsApp messages from Rick checking on me and one from Chuck telling me that his connection from Abu Dhabi is delayed. This good news means that Chuck's flight into Kathmandu will be touching down around the same time as mine.

The original plan was to meet at the Newa Chen Hotel in Kathmandu before heading into the mountains. Now we will be able to find one another at the airport and catch a taxi to the hotel together. I had been bracing to deal with a chaotic scrum for an airport taxi all by myself. In Nepal, I had been warned, people don't line up by western standards; there is a lot of jostling and bargaining to get a taxi.

I hurry down several long hallways with posters displaying the iconic peak of Mount Everest set against an impossibly blue sky. "Welcome to Nepal" they announce in English. My goal is to move quickly through the Arrivals Terminal to beat the long lines that can keep you waiting for hours at the immigration desk. I have printed out my 30-day visa application ahead of time, so I am able to bypass the electric terminals that frustrate many travelers. I line up at the Visa Fee Collection Counter under a sign that says "15-30 Days" and hand in my paperwork along with $40, making me one of the first visitors through immigration.

My hustle to get through immigration doesn't matter much given how the polyglot of humanity begins to swell at Baggage Claim. More flights land, including Chuck's connection from Abu Dhabi.

"Hello, mate," I call out with a big smile when I finally see Chuck descend the stairs into Baggage Claim.

Looking fit and in good humor following two flights, Chuck is wearing a gray shirt and zip-off gray pants, the kind hikers use to turn trousers into shorts. Like me, he is carrying only his daypack after checking his bigger backpack and walking poles. His eyes crinkle when he smiles, and his white hair is shorter than I remember.

"We made it!"

We are both excited to be on the ground in Nepal after so much planning and so many travel miles. A sense of wholehearted anticipation for the journey ahead pulses through me. Chuck and I check in with each other, asking about our families and sharing recent news related to the trip. I ask him if he heard about the recent earthquake and he shakes his head. We settle in for a long and crowded wait for our bags to arrive.

Two hours pass, and my initial shot of adrenaline fades. I realize I am bone tired but perk up when I see my backpack on the conveyor belt ahead. I whisper a little prayer of thanks.

I then understand why we have waited so long for our bags to offload. I have never seen the hodgepodge of items that roll through the flaps. There are electronic goods ranging from flat screen TVs and toasters to music systems that were purchased in countries where consumer goods are plentiful. Overstuffed duffel bags and shrink-wrapped suitcases circle the carousel. I chat with two young Nepali men standing nearby who are waiting for bottles of Spanish wine, chorizo sausage, and the western clothes they are bringing as gifts to a wedding.

Finally, Chuck and I have our packs and exit Baggage Claim. Outside the airport doors, taxi drivers press towards us, shouting and vying for our attention. After a bit of intense bargaining, we wrangle a taxi at a much higher price than we had expected to pay. Nepal is experiencing a serious gas shortage, the result of a blockade on the border with India that has virtually halted the movement of essential goods between the two countries. Our trck requires us to take taxi and bus rides to get from the Kathmandu Valley into the Himalayas. This is the first sign of how fuel shortages will add to our costs and complicate our ability to travel in a country with an already poor and primitive infrastructure.

Chuck and I bounce along dark and deeply rutted streets during a 30-minute ride to the Newa Chen. Chuck had selected the Newa Chen so that we could stay in a traditional Newari lodge in a historical section of the valley. I can't see much of the city on the drive, but I am struck by the darkness outside the van. There are no neon signs, no lights in windows, just dim headlights and the occasional streetlight that fades from sight as we bump farther away from the airport. It is only 10 p.m., but the capital city seems eerily empty. The shadows of a few people appear and disappear amid shapes that scurry by. My eyes widen to make out packs of wild dogs running through the streets. I think, "Oh, my God, where am I?" These fighting packs of canines make me feel as if I am in a dystopian world, one where wild animals rule the night.

The street dogs and strays of Nepal are legendary. On the streets of Kathmandu alone, there are more than 20,000 dogs that savagely protect their turf. Locals and visitors alike must be careful not to tangle with the dogs. Periodically, Nepal tries to cull the massive population and reduce the number of dog bites that people suffer daily. But animal rights protests and the Nepali love of dogs largely put an end to the mass killing of street dogs several years ago. I take a quick mental inventory of my vaccinations, reminding myself that my rabies shot is up to date.

The Newa Chen turns out to be a peaceful refuge near Patan Durbar Square. No wonder the ride here has taken so long. We are quite far away from the center of the capital. Most tourists stay in an area of Kathmandu called Thamel, where the hotels and restaurants cater to foreign travelers. Our traditional Newari hotel is in Lalitpur, the oldest of the three cities situated in the sprawling Kathmandu Valley. This is the home of ancient Hindu and Buddhist temples, a former royal palace, and sacred shrines, many of which lie in crumbled piles of bricks from the quake.

The door of the Newa Chen opens and Chuck and I are warmly greeted with "Namaste," the traditional Nepali welcome. After downing a cup of masala chai tea, I am off to bed, with earplugs to block out the barking and baying of the dogs outside my window, for my first real shuteye in two days.

Chapter 4

BECAUSE I'M CURIOUS

Throughout my career, I have worked for several members of Congress, one cabinet secretary, a governor, and four CEOs. I've always been interested in what sets leaders apart. Some are clearly driven by power, ego, and money. Servant leaders, on the other hand, want to make a difference and leave their communities a better place. All these leaders, whether commercial, political, or community-based, share an attribute important in a world of disruption and rapid change. You might think that this trait must be all about self-confidence, conviction, or resilience. I believe it is more about curiosity. Curiosity may not help you predict the future, but it certainly fuels your willingness to lean into ambiguity and experiment with what is new and novel. You can't stand still and be curious at the same time.

> *I think, at a child's birth, if a mother could ask a fairy godmother to endow it with the most useful gift, that gift should be curiosity.*
> ~ Eleanor Roosevelt

I was curious about seeing a new part of the world and testing whether I was fit enough to take a walk in the Himalayas. This was not about scaling Mount Everest—I wasn't deluding myself that I was now capable of mountain climbing—but about trekking a popular walking route in a remote corner of the world. While I had not aspired to walk the Annapurna Circuit in the past, when given the opportunity I was curious about what I would find. We're all curious about something.

Only in the rearview mirror do I see my pattern of using travel—not vacationing, mind you, but adventure travel—to transition to my next step in life. Thirty years ago, when I moved from Washington, D.C. to Pennsylvania, it took me three months of traveling in Mexico to get there. How odd to travel south to land north. I lived with Mexican host families and studied the Spanish language in small institutes in Mexico. As I wandered along the Gringo Trail, climbing the steps of Mexico's ancient Mayan ruins, and wandering through its colonial past, I sorted out my plans for the future. I was in my twenties and in transition. Mexico offered an opportunity to reset my course and explore a new country at the same time. Curiosity combined with a longing to try something new seems to be hard-wired into my sense of identity.

And again, when I left my position in the grocery industry, I used walking across Spain with Juliet as a way of stepping away from the distractions of my day-to-day life. I cleared my calendar so I could clean my slate and begin writing a new chapter based on what I wanted to do next. I just needed to figure out what that was.

Now, I am in yet another new country with a whole different set of sights, sounds, and traditions. Once again, I am on a quest for answers in a faraway place, turning my world upside-down to look at my life from a new perspective. After all my research into the Annapurna Circuit, I figure I'm pretty clear about the challenges. In some ways, I want to be here because of the challenges.

Nepal is home to many ethnicities, and our neighborhood of Patan is in the heart of the Newari people, famous as the artisans and architects who built the world-famous Patan Durbar Square. Considered some of the oldest inhabitants of the Kathmandu Valley, the Newars are an ethnic mix of Indian, Tibetan, and Burmese. They practice a combination of Hinduism and Buddhism. I will see this peaceful coexistence between different religions many times over in Nepal. Often the same temples are used for the worship of several different religions. There appears to be no animus between religious beliefs; in fact, they mix and intermingle with an ancient and easy kinship.

Chuck and I sit in the courtyard of the Newa Chen enjoying an al fresco breakfast of fruit, naan, and hard-boiled eggs. In the corner of the courtyard, the owner's wife tends to a small offering of incense, oranges, and marigolds. Together, Chuck and I plan a day exploring the warren of streets around the hotel. While we will be on foot all day, there is plenty to see nearby, including the painstaking clean-up and restoration of Patan Durbar Square.

Outside of the peaceful refuge of the Newa Chen, the streets are congested with people, potholes, and sleeping dogs resting up for their nighttime scavenging. Vendors display their wares on bedsheets and milk crates. Calvin Klein briefs and children's pajamas are displayed next to a folding table of raw meat buzzing with flies. A mass of enormous balloons walks by, hiding the boy carrying them, and a woman in a colorful sari pushes a bicycle hung with baskets of plastic cookware.

The noise and commotion shock my senses. Chuck and I, as Westerners, are greeted on the streets with smiles and nods but are largely left alone to explore. We fill the day ambling past elaborate shrines adorned with offerings of flowers and fruit, and peek into courtyards filled with Buddhas and prayer wheels.

One courtyard is the home of a young girl who is thought to be a living goddess. This goddess, called a Kumari, is worshipped as a living symbol of the divine female. Top government officials visit her for blessings and predictions, and she is paid a stipend by the Nepali government in recognition of her special powers. But this is not a lifetime gig. Once the young Kumari has her first period, a new goddess must be found. Ancient rituals are alive and well in the Kathmandu Valley and, after an elaborate selection process, powers are transferred to a new Kumari, sometimes a girl as young as one-and-a-half years old.

Believers visit the courtyard where we stand, hoping that the goddess might pull aside a curtain from her window. We don't see the reclusive Kumari this day, which is too bad, since even a glimpse of her red clothes and the fire eye painted on her forehead is believed to bring good fortune. I have mixed emotions about how a little girl can be worshipped as a goddess until she reaches puberty, at which time she becomes mortal once again. I travel to learn and appreciate different cultures, so I try not to judge.

Back out on the street, I step over a flattened rat just as a bus of uniformed schoolkids pulls up to unload. Looking tidy in their white button-downs and starched uniforms, the students laugh and kid with each other as they climb down from on top of the bus. I can't imagine emerging that clean after riding on the roof of the bus. I don't know it at the time but, in a few short weeks, I will be fighting my own battle for cleanliness.

The fuel shortage is taking its toll on the capital. Long lines of motor bikes are parked in the streets. They have been queued up for several days waiting for gas. Their young owners—all Nepali men—take turns sleeping and guarding their bikes until the gas station receives a new supply of petrol, at which time they can fill up and be on their way.

This also means that taxis are hard to find. A longer tour of the expansive Kathmandu Valley will need to wait until tomorrow when we meet with a local man, Karma Sherpa, who works for an American friend of mine named Steve. Steve and I worked in the same congressional office in the 1980s. His career took an interesting turn away from politics, and today he and his wife run a business importing fabric from India and Nepal. They turn these colorful textiles into expensive satchels and purses that are sold at high-end stores such as Neiman Marcus.

I have never heard of anyone named Karma and wonder, but don't ask, if Karma is a Western translation of a more complicated Nepali name. How rude to inquire, "Is that really your name?" So I don't.

Karma is from the Sherpa ethnic group. If you go far enough back in history, the Sherpas came from Tibet, bringing their Buddhist beliefs with them and settling in the Himalayan region of Nepal. They are famous as mountaineers and for transporting inhuman loads on their backs at high altitudes. The generic term "sherpa" has even become a verb, as in "to sherpa a heavy load." Sherpa Tenzing Norgay, the first Nepali to climb Mount Everest with Sir Edmund Hillary, is regarded as one of the country's national heroes.

Sherpas have facial features that look more Tibetan than Indian, providing a clear physical distinction between them and the ethnic groups that live in the lowlands. The smooth skin on Karma's

clean-shaven face makes him look like a young 20-
something, but his dark, wise-looking eyes and calm
demeanor convey an older, more experienced man in
his 30s. A skilled mountain guide, Karma guided
Steve and his family to Everest Base Camp several
years ago and has worked as an in-country contact for
their textile business ever since.

Karma Sherpa and his private driver pick us up at
10 a.m. for a full-day tour of the sights of Kathmandu.
The fuel shortage makes it difficult to scare up a taxi.
In fact, we never could have done it on our own. Our
first stop is Pashupatinath Temple, a holy Hindu site
teeming with rhesus monkeys and Hindu temples. As
we walk around the grounds of the shrine, we take a
few photos with the smiling sadhus who, for a
contribution, pose and bless us with a tika, a mark of
red powder on our foreheads. These holy men make
a living painting their faces and smiling for tourist
photos. I put rupees in their cup and accept all the
blessings I can get.

Along the banks of a tributary of the river Ganges,
Hindu funeral pyres are cremating the recently
deceased. Two bonfires are smoking and giving off
an odd smell. A man wades in the water as two boys
splash each other alongside the pyres. Overlooking
the scene, I experience a moment of cultural con-
fusion as I watch families bathing, washing, and
playing in the water with the remains of dead loved
ones drifting by.

We climb to the top of the hill for a view that fans out across the expanse of Kathmandu. Monkeys keep a watchful eye on us from building ledges while Karma helps Chuck and I buy a string of Tibetan prayer flags from a boy selling trinkets. Hanging from the string are colored squares that repeat first blue, then white, red, green, and yellow, altogether representing a balance of the earth's elements.

For a small fee, a resident monk at the temple blesses our flags. Just beyond the young boy, the temple's resident monk sits cross-legged in a makeshift tent and, for a small fee, blesses our flags. We watch as he chants, sprinkles holy water, and throws grains of rice on our flags.

This is a symbolic moment for me. The plan is to hang the flags at the top of the Thorung La pass in roughly two weeks' time. Having a monk consecrate the flags seems like a promising act of faith, as though his personal blessing for good fortune is a sign of approval and ultimate success.

Finally, it is time for an end-of-the-day beer in Thamel, the district best known to tourists and trekkers. Sitting in the Jesse James bar, Karma Sherpa reviews what we know of our route and provides valuable tips for the trek. According to Karma, the Annapurna region was not hit hard by the earthquake, not like the destruction in the Everest area where Karma's family lives. I am flooded with excitement as we gear up for tomorrow's flight to Pokhara, a lakeside resort at the foot of the Annapurnas where we will meet our guide, Bhimsen, and finally get walking.

The following day, our Yeti Air flight is delayed due to rain and fog, but we eventually make our way to Pokhara, Nepal's second-largest city and a jumping-off point for various mountain adventures. French, Germans, and a group of young Americans from Colorado stand in their hiking boots as we wait to disembark from our 45-minute flight. Some of them have come to trek into the Annapurna Massif, heading to the Annapurna Circuit, like us, or to Poon Hill. Others arrive in harem pants, flip flops, and dreadlocks, ready for their yoga retreats. I'm ready too.

Chapter 5

PLOT TWIST

The Trek-o-Tel is situated at one end of Pokhara's main drag overlooking Phewa Lake. I've seldom seen a more stunning backdrop with the lake in the foreground and the Himalayas rising behind it. A sunny day makes everything appear in high relief. The Trek-o-Tel's garden is lit up with orange, pink, and purple blossoms all nestled against a lush background, at its peak of green following the rainy season.

Inside, the hotel is a bit worn around the edges, but it clearly caters to European and American guests. When the British colonized India, they took their china and furnishings with them to feel at home. The westernized surroundings of the Trek-o-Tel make me feel more at home than I have since I landed in Nepal four days ago. I have no idea that these feelings of familiarity are about to end abruptly.

The restaurants that back up to Phewa Lake have names like Be Happy, Utopia Garden, Monsoon, and Moondance. They overlook a walking path that provides access to small piers and boating ramps. Motorized boats are not allowed on the lake, but an array of colorful rowboats is tethered along the shoreline to ferry visitors to a shrine that emerges like an illusion from the middle of the lake. Looking down the length of the lake, I can see the striking spire of Machapuchare (Fish Tail), which is among the highest peaks in the world and, at this writing, still in the record books for having never been summited.

Men and women have set out from Pokhara on expeditions with much more strenuous climbs than mine ahead of them. Still, I am here in Nepal on an expedition of my own. It's a type of travel that demands a huge heap of commitment. The anticipation of setting out on an expedition is both exciting and terrifying. The fact that there is a personal goal involved makes it difficult to abandon, even when careful planning falls short. I congratulate myself for being on an expedition. Once again, a feeling of focused determination settles into my psyche.

That determination—to go on, to see it through, to make it work—is just what you need when you are forced to make a change of plans. Life teaches you—and travel has a way of underscoring this point—that a certain amount of flexibility is required. Sometimes a change in plans can lead to an even better outcome, one that you didn't initially consider. You just don't know that at the time. I certainly didn't know as I began my expedition that my adaptability would be tested in the face of a big change of plans.

Waiting in the garden of the Trek-o-Tel, Chuck tells the story of how he met Bhimsen when he trekked to the Annapurna Sanctuary on his earlier visit.

"I was introduced to Bhimsen by a friend who worked in peace-building for the Nepali government," Chuck relates. "Locally, he is known as a man of iron, a skilled and energetic guide who taught himself excellent English and Japanese in order to accommodate his walking clients."

On that trek, a member of Chuck's party suffered from altitude sickness and had to be taken urgently to lower ground.

"When it became obvious that Patrick was suffering from fairly severe mountain sickness, Bhimsen and I had to bring him down," Chuck recounts. "It took us more than four hours to descend 2,000 feet on a rough mountain path in complete darkness."

The man recovered, and Chuck trusts Bhimsen based upon his handling of this life-threatening emergency high in the Himalayas. If Chuck trusts Bhimsen, so do I.

When Chuck and I were preparing for the trip, I asked how much money I should budget for the guide and lodging. On his previous trip, Chuck had spent $15 a day for his guided trek to the Annapurna Sanctuary, a price negotiated by their mutual friend. But communications with Bhimsen had been difficult before our trip and Chuck didn't have a firm price.

Bhimsen checked emails occasionally on a computer in the next village. There was no Wi-Fi for WhatsApp calls, so all we knew was that we would meet Bhimsen on Monday at 9 a.m. to sort out our final plans.

Since Chuck's last visit to Nepal had been a few years ago, he'd suggested we double the daily amount he'd spent, to be safe. I budgeted $30 a day when I ordered my stack of Nepali rupees for the trip.

And now here he is. Bhimsen appears on the grounds of the Trek-o-Tel after walking two hours from his remote hill village. As he approaches, I see an older man with close-cropped gray hair, a weathered face, and a small, wizened build. He is accompanied by two lean young men.

Bhimsen looks directly at us when he says, "I am old, and my knees are bad. I will not be walking with you into the mountains. Meet my nephew, Ganesh. He will guide you."

Before we can process the fact that we will not be guided by someone Chuck knows and trusts, Bhimsen turns in his flip-flops and begins his two-hour journey back home.

And just like that he is gone, disappearing from the Trek-o-Tel's garden.

I haven't been struck speechless too many times in my life. I have made a career out of always finding the words and never letting shock show on my face. Now I wonder if my mouth is hanging open in disbelief.

Handed the baton, Ganesh takes over the conversation and introduces his porter, Moti. Both men look to be in their early thirties, fit and capable. Ganesh speaks good English; Moti, not so much. As the four of us sit down on the terrace to discuss our plans, I can't help but feel that there has been a bait-and-switch and that the spotty communication had been contrived by Bhimsen so as not to lose a valuable guiding gig along with the scarce income it meant, not only for his family, but also for the entire village.

Beginning a relationship with a less-than-honest start is hard enough in any circumstance. Beginning it with someone I need to trust for my personal safety puts me back on my heels. Chuck and I are both taken totally off guard by Bhimsen's abrupt departure. I swallow a heavy dollop of suspicion; it tastes like vinegar in my mouth.

But Ganesh is clearly a confident and experienced guide. We get to know each other over the next four hours as we map the route and fill out forms to obtain the necessary permits to walk in the Annapurnas. Trekkers need a basic permit issued by the Nepal Tourism Board and the Trekking Agencies Association of Nepal to ensure the safety and security of every trekker. In addition, the Annapurna region is the largest protected conservation area in Nepal, which requires us to purchase an Annapurna Conservation Area Entry Permit and a TIMS card before setting out. The Trekker's Information Management

System, or TIMS, card provides a centralized database that aids in rescue operations and emergencies when trekkers are at risk.

In the Hindu religion, Ganesh is a god of wisdom, success, and good luck. I don't know this at the time, but I calm myself down, ask professional questions, and try to regain my footing. Ganesh is a husband and a father. When he isn't guiding trekkers—which is not often lately—he makes a hardscrabble living farming the land. Like the promise of spring, my sense of security and trust in Ganesh begins to bud and show itself.

Finally, the conversation turns to money. How much will our route to the turnaround point of Jomsom cost us each day?

"The going rate is $150 a day," Ganesh tells us.

$150 a day? Each? Chuck and I are shocked. While I had doubled the estimated $15 a day and brought with me a safe supply of additional rupees beyond that, this is all the money I have. Ganesh and Moti take a walk while Chuck and I process this staggering news. Despite our careful planning, neither of us is prepared for this surprise.

"How could we not know that the going rate is $150 a day?" I ask with too much accusation in my voice. I am as angry with myself as I am with anyone. Not knowing what things cost on the ground, or at least in the ballpark, feels like an avoidable mistake.

"Clearly the earthquake has made all kinds of things in Nepal more difficult and more expensive," replies Chuck, also clearly baffled by this new information. "We know that the boycott on the border is driving black market prices for all kinds of things."

"I have the cash," I confirm. "But it's just about all I have."

"I will need to withdraw money," says Chuck. "But I didn't come all this way to turn back now."

"You have a decision to make as well," he tells me. But I've already made up my mind.

This is not a hard decision for me. I trained for months and flew nearly 8,000 miles from home to trek the world-famous Annapurna Circuit in Nepal. Once I satisfy myself about the fact that Ganesh will be our guide, the cost is not a game-changer for me. If the "going rate" is $150 a day, well, we have little choice but to pay.

This is one of the many times during this adventure when I had to take stock of my decisions and ask myself, "Okay, Tracy, how much do you want this?" The opportunities to turn back—and without any shame—keep presenting themselves. Just like in life when we stand at a turning point, we need to check in with ourselves and decide which way to go. But making a course correction when you need to is not always easy. People who are highly adaptable may be better able to reconcile themselves to their new circumstances, but it still takes work. God seems to be testing my ability to stay positive and clear-headed in the moment.

Ganesh needs half of the payment up front to make arrangements and pay for our permits. Chuck takes a quick walk to visit several ATMs in order to make his cash payment. I make small talk with the men while he is gone, asking about their families and what they grow in their fields. I learn that life is harder than ever after the earthquake. There are few tourists and fewer treks. While the price I need to pay is much higher than I had planned, I am happy to contribute to the local economy and the ability of these two men to support themselves and their families.

Just before lunch, we say goodbye to Ganesh and Moti. Emotionally drained by the whole affair, Chuck and I agree to spend the afternoon doing our own thing. Before saying goodbye, we arrange to regroup for dinner early that evening.

Chapter 6

NEGOTIATING A NEW DEAL

That afternoon, I walk along the main street in Pokhara, past guest houses and shops filled with cheap souvenirs, colorful pashminas, and knock-off outdoor gear. Open storefronts advertise travel and trekking services with English-speaking guides. At 23,000 feet, Fish Tail appears to gaze down at her reflection in the still, glassy lake. The painted wooden rowboats lined up along the lakefront look like a postcard; for-hire signs beckon passersby to visit the island temple. No doubt about it. This is an exceptionally beautiful place.

When Chuck and I meet at 6 p.m. to walk to dinner, Chuck tells me that we have another decision to make. His Irish blood is boiling.

"I spent the afternoon visiting the trekking agencies in town," he says. "The going rate is not $150 a day. It's $70 a day. We've been buggered."

I had also stopped in at various trekking agencies and had been told the same information: $70 a day.

Sitting in an open-air Chinese restaurant eating chicken fried noodles, Chuck shares his idea to report Ganesh to the tourist police.

"I plan to use my phone to get Ganesh on tape telling us that the going rate is $150," says my Irish friend. First the deceptive bait-and-switch on guides, now the price. I think of that old saying, "Fool me once, shame on you. Fool me twice, shame on me."

My crisis communications training kicks in. In my line of business, you learn early not to escalate a situation before you can see where it is going. You match your response to the crisis at hand, weigh it against what is unfolding at the time, and step it up as the situation worsens if, in fact, it does. Sometimes initial measures are enough. Think of it as keeping your powder dry so that you have enough powder available if you need to fire back.

I am not ready to ruin Ganesh's reputation, but I also am not prepared to go into the mountains with a guide I don't fully trust. What will the backlash be if we threaten to turn Ganesh in to the authorities? We are in a foreign country 8,000 miles from home. I'm not really afraid for our personal safety—Ganesh doesn't seem like the threatening type—but I don't know what might happen next. I also worry about what such a big black mark would mean for Ganesh and his ability to provide for his family. Would our actions bring dishonor and shame to these men?

Over dinner, Chuck and I devise a plan. Ganesh and Moti are scheduled to pick us up at 9 a.m. the next morning, at which time we will ask for our money back. Chuck and I will offer the men several hundred dollars for their time and trouble. If Ganesh refuses to refund the rest of our down payment, we can go to the tourist police and escalate the situation at that time.

While I am satisfied with our plan, I still sleep fitfully that night.

Promptly at 9 a.m. the next morning, Ganesh and Moti arrive in a taxi they have hired for the three-hour ride to Besisahar. Chuck and I invite the men to the terrace for coffee before we depart. When we sit down, Chuck begins.

"Yesterday you told us that the going rate for a guide on the circuit is $150 a day. I visited at least six agencies, and the going rate is $70 a day."

"I don't know how that can be," replies Ganesh. He is rattled. "Prices are very high due to the lack of fuel in the mountains and the festival."

I pick up the conversation from Chuck, just as we had discussed the night before. "Ganesh," I say, "This is an issue of trust for me. I am not prepared to walk into the mountains with a guide I cannot trust. Chuck and I talked about it and we want you to give us our money back and hand over our permits. We want to give you and Moti $200 for your time and effort."

"But I don't have your money."

"Where is it?" I ask.

"It's in my village."

Had Ganesh and Moti already given the money to their families for the festival? What if the money is already gone? The entire country is provisioning for nearly two weeks of holiday. If food is scarce, maybe these two men just salvaged the holiday by bringing back a sizable sum of money to fund their village's celebrations.

I have to think fast.

"Is there any reason you can't take the taxi waiting at the curb back to your village and return with our money?" I ask, keeping my tone level. "Moti can wait here with us as a gesture of good faith."

Ganesh is torn and tries to talk us out of a decision that has already been made. He speaks to Moti in Nepalese, asking him to stay behind. Before leaving, he says he wants to leave his backpack with us as well. That way, we will know that he is coming back. When Chuck asks how long he will be, he says he will return in two hours with our money.

For the next two hours, Chuck and I sit in the garden with Moti. His English is limited but his disappointment is clear.

Moti believes that he will never see any of the $200 we have given to Ganesh for the both of them. "We will tell Ganesh to pay you," I try to reassure him. But porters work for guides and we are not willing to circumvent the hierarchy. We have to hope that Ganesh will pay Moti for the time he spent with us yesterday and today.

There is never a question that Ganesh will return. We have Moti and we have Ganesh's backpack. So when the taxi pulls back up around noon, Ganesh walks over to the three of us in the garden. He hands our money back and we count out $200. Remembering the conversation with Moti, I remind Ganesh to share a portion with his porter and he promises that he will. We thank them and say goodbye.

After Ganesh and Moti leave, I sit on the stone terrace overlooking the Trek-o-Tel's lush garden and cry. As I untangle my emotions, I don't know if I am more upset about the betrayal I feel, or the realization of how difficult life is for these Nepali men. If Ganesh had truly padded his fee, I can't blame him for trying. It's possible that yesterday Ganesh and Moti returned to their homes as heroes, earning enough money for the village to celebrate the festival and perhaps providing for months to come. What did they tell their families today when they returned almost empty-handed? Did they lie to save face?

I blame myself for not being well enough informed to negotiate a more favorable rate before mistrust changed the game. Shaking off my regret, I ask myself once again, "Okay, Tracy, how much do you want this? Will you turn back or continue?"

I didn't come all this way not to adapt to a new set of circumstances. We know our next steps. After taking a short break to gather our thoughts, Chuck and I walk down the main street ready to negotiate a new deal.

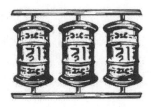

───────── Chapter 7 ─────────

ON A SEESAW OF EMOTION

When I handled crisis communications for a major grocery store chain, it was my responsibility to gauge what degree of a crisis we might be experiencing and how serious the risk was to the company's reputation. I had to see around the corner as to where an issue or event might be headed. Was it a blip on the screen or a threat to the stock price? This wasn't my job alone, but it was a big part of my role. Week after week was filled with events you just can't make up, everything from food safety scares and violent crimes on the property to employee disputes and a wide range of naughtiness in the parking lot.

One day I was driving down the highway after a store visit when my cell phone rang. On the other end was an investigative reporter I knew inquiring about a brick of cocaine discovered in a flower shipment from the country of Colombia. Could I confirm?

I had no intention of having that conversation while I was driving down the highway. "I'll need to get back to you on that."

"Thirteen ounces of cocaine were found on Monday in a shipment of flowers in your distribution center. You mean you don't know about this?" She tried to make me appear out-of-the-loop.

"Kate, I'll need to get back to you."

Of course I knew about it. I had known about it since the cocaine was discovered when the shipment of flowers was unpacked the previous week. Our team had done everything right, including reporting the incident to the State Police, but I wasn't about to confirm a story before I checked on its status and investigated how the reporter had gotten all the facts. Because she had all the facts. Plus, you don't answer these questions on the fly. My job was to protect the company's reputation. Would people question whether our flower shipments regularly contained illicit drugs? Were our Colombian flower suppliers also cocaine dealers? A story like this can break in different ways, so it was my job to answer questions in a way that helped the media get the story right. When it finally was reported, our warehouse team looked like the heroes they were for taking quick action and calling the authorities.

How many times did I get a call about a customer complaint of a dead black widow spider found in a bag of grapes? Their signature red hourglass-shaped marking makes them easy to identify. Everyone who hears about this wants to know how common it is to find a poisonous spider in the produce section. Black widows like to nest in the warm, protected center of a grape cluster. It's more common than you think. One day, the black widow spider discovered was still alive and was donated by the customer and her kids to the insect exhibit at a local zoo. I appreciated their sense of humor. My comment was to remind customers that a decreasing use of pesticides some-times results in unwanted squatters so it's advisable to inspect and wash your grapes before eating them.

In more rural locations, it wasn't unheard of to have a terrified deer run through the front doors of a store during hunting season, knocking over displays until the store team could finally herd the poor animal to the exit. There was a big clean-up in the aisles after those incidents.

An upsetting call came to me one winter day. A man had been stabbed in the bathroom of one of our stores. Of course, the police were called, and I learned that several local reporters, who follow the police frequencies, were outside the store. I wanted to know first things first: was the man okay? Yes, it was a flesh wound, but he fell out of his wheelchair. He had been in a wheelchair? Yes. Did they catch the culprit? Yes, she was not happy with her payment. Her payment? Yes, she was apparently turning a trick in the store bathroom. Too bad the official statement couldn't include the reminder, "Hey, people, use the bathroom for what it's intended!"

Product recalls were typically issued late on Fridays, meaning that there were few Friday happy hours for me. Instead, my team would be alerting the media and calling customers to let them know that they might have purchased a recalled product. Our commitment to maintaining a trusted relationship with our customers was always in the forefront of our minds, giving people accurate and timely information so that they could act accordingly. Customers told us how much they appreciated and respected us for these efforts to communicate bad news and be clear about what we were doing to respond.

But there were times that we just couldn't win. The company had a policy that prohibited charitable organizations from soliciting customers for donations on their way into stores. Think Salvation Army bell ringers and the Girl Scouts selling their cookies. Since they weren't allowed to ask our customers for money or sell them their cookies, popcorn, flower seeds, or Christmas wreaths, the company made generous contributions to these organizations and explained that the policy had nothing to do with the merits of their charity. When we acquired a chain of grocery stores south of the Mason-Dixon Line, a chain that had permitted these solicitations, it was my job to let the community know that things had changed. There was a new policy in place. Most of the charities were understanding and gracious. But not all of them. Not the Girl Scouts.

And so I found my name in the pages of the community newspaper under the headline, "Making little girls cry." Customers called to complain, and I called every one of them back personally. One man, who had heard me on the radio earlier that day, accused me of being un-American.

There were also human rights protests outside the corporate office about the price we had paid for tomatoes. The unions called us "corporate rats" and wheeled Scabby, a gigantic, inflatable rat, into the parking lot of our unionized stores during testy labor negotiations. Each Christmas there was a debate about whether our cashiers could wish customers a Merry Christmas and Happy Hanukkah or whether that would alienate the non-believers.

"We're just trying to sell groceries here!"

People bring all kinds of issues into their neighborhood market, a place that you don't typically think of as a hotbed for controversy. These issues taught me how to be careful and fast at the same time. When I coach clients and executives about how to react in a crisis, I remind them that it's easy to be careful and it's easy to be fast. Being both at the same time requires training, experience, and confidence. Reacting in the moment requires a quick scan of the facts as you know them at the time—facts that are always incomplete—and a sure-footed decision on next steps.

Of all the traits required to make a solid decision in the moment, understanding the lens through which you look may be the most important. Perspective… are you playing defense and back on your heels, responding to what comes flying over the transom? Do you understand what is driving the issue in the first place? Are you scared and making decisions driven by fear? Or are you on the balls of your feet and leaning into whatever direction you need to go? I would calm my staff down by reminding them, "It's not world peace and no one is going to die. Unless, of course, it is world peace, and someone could die." Most of the time it's not, and your ability to remain clear-headed and trust your gut in moments of uncertainty drives how confident you are in the next steps you take.

Chuck and I walk into the Pristine Mountain Adventure office in Pokhara hoping to begin our trek on the Annapurna Circuit the next day. We pick the Pristine agency for no particular reason except that it is open and is one of the storefronts Chuck had visited the day before. Two men sit at desks in the office, one in the front room and another in a cramped office just beyond an open doorway. The men are anxious to accommodate our every need, answering our questions and flying into action to make the arrangements. One man runs down a list of guides while the other calls porters on his mobile phone. Many have already returned to their home villages to celebrate Dashain with their families. Nearly two hours pass before they can assemble our team. But assemble a team they do, with 47-year-old Ram as our guide, and 21-year-old Som as our porter.

Both men are called to the agency to meet with us. Ram walks through the door with a quiet but capable countenance. He is an experienced guide who has led trekkers into the mountains for more than 20 years. He wears a gray baseball hat on a slightly balding head and looks at us through wire-frame glasses. Ram is not much taller than I; his slight, wiry build is well-suited for scrambling up the side of the mountain, as we will soon learn.

Som arrives a few minutes later on his motorbike. He looks like a handsome Nepali movie star, with straight black hair that falls across aviator Ray-Bans. Removing his glasses to reveal big brown eyes and a full round face, he introduces himself with an easy smile and tells us in broken English how pleased he is to meet us.

Both these men live in Pokhara. As Hindus, it is festival time for them too, but work is scarce, so they are enthusiastic about the trek. It doesn't take long to establish a quick rapport and finalize our plans to begin walking the next day, only one day behind schedule.

Our new arrangements are a cause to celebrate. Chuck and I have dinner at an Italian pizza place that caters to foreigners. The disappointment of the last two days hangs between us but is offset by our eagerness to put our early misadventures behind us. I am still feeling conflicted about whether this trek is going to work out. My emotional seesaw is first up and then down. Are these changes in our plans an even better option or just a new plan? Is Ganesh a good guy or a bad guy? Is every step we take going to offer a whole new set of problems to solve? Is this trip supposed to be fun or frightening? These questions keep my emotions rising and falling, pitching me from optimism to the other end of the spectrum, a place I'll call dread, making it hard to find my balance.

"Chuck, shouldn't we have known the price of the trek before arriving?" I thought about how easy it was to confirm the price once we started asking around. "Couldn't all of this have been avoided?" I ask.

Trying not to be too defensive and succeeding only half of the time, Chuck is honest in saying that this has put a strain on our friendship.

"You have to decide how you feel about things, including our friendship," he replies.

At that moment, it dawns on me that we are traveling companions and equals. While it was natural for me to think about this as Chuck's expedition; in reality, Chuck and I are two travelers on a common path, both in control of our own decisions and destinies. Like an "aha" moment, I realize that I am responsible for the outcome of my experience in Nepal. I embrace the challenges and remind myself that I wanted to be here in part *because* of the challenges.

> *It is not the mountain we conquer, but ourselves.*
>
> ~ Sir Edmund Hillary

As we leave the restaurant, rain from a heavy downpour is running fast and is already a foot deep in Pokhara's main street. The monsoon-like rain makes me wonder about the potential for rockslides and deteriorating conditions in the mountains. I banish those thoughts and try to shake the fact that I am turning everything that happens into a bigger worry than it needs to be. "It is not the mountain we conquer, but ourselves," I repeat.

We wade across the street and stop in a small shop so that I can buy a hemp hat woven by Nepali women. The shop advertises that these women are paid a fair wage, giving me a little boost of energy and good vibes.

Earlier in the day, Chuck and I had switched from the Trek-o-Tel to the Hotel Tulsi, maybe to signify a fresh start. The power is out at the Hotel Tulsi. In fact, the power has been out since we checked in. Rolling power outages are common here, and the day's late-season storm only added to the stress on the electric grid. As I pack my gear for the next day, I wear my headlamp. I can't charge my portable battery, but it still has a few days of life in it. I will charge it wherever I can along the trek.

I'm in the dark with only a dim light to find my way. It should come as no surprise that I keep stubbing my toe on the bed frame as I move around the hotel room. The metaphor is not lost on me.

Like stepping out of the dark, both literally and figuratively, the morning gives way to clear skies and the promise of a new day. We stow our extra gear in the hotel's luggage room and sign a form saying we will return for it fifteen days later. Ram and Som meet us outside the hotel with smiles and good cheer. The streets are dry and there is no sign of the flooding from the night before. I tuck away the unease of the last several days and get excited about beginning to walk.

The three-hour taxi ride to Besisahar provides the opportunity to see village life in Nepal. The road is paved, but where the pavement has been washed out, it is dusty and deeply pocked with potholes. Our driver takes this in stride and deftly avoids the rocks and ruts when he can. But most of the time, there is no room to maneuver around the breaks and bumps in the pavement. The road is jam-packed with an incongruous jumble of people, animals, and vehicles. My front-seat vantage point gives me a clear view of swaying buses groaning with people, colorfully painted trucks, bicycles, and motorbikes. There are schoolkids in uniform and pedestrians walking in the street and groups of people standing around waiting. For a bus? A ride? I don't know. Cows amble across the road, and everywhere there are dogs, sometimes sleeping in the middle of the street, oblivious to the chaos unfolding around them. I wonder where all these people and animals are going and if the crowds are related to the festival or if this is just everyday life in Nepal.

Our taxi driver loads a cassette tape, and we jam to traditional Nepali music mixed with Rod Stewart classics as he and Ram chat in English about Nepali politics. The driver is a former trekking guide, but he tells Ram that guiding didn't provide enough money to support his wife and four children in the off-season, especially since the earthquake. He wears a traditional Nepali hat, a brimless topi, a spotless button-down shirt, and trousers. Once again, I wonder how he looks so clean; I've been in Nepal for only five days and I'm already feeling grimy.

As I listen to the eclectic choice of music and their discussion about politics, I get my head around my first days in Nepal. It hasn't been an easy start. Reviewing each new set of circumstances forces me to rethink plans, wrestle with my feelings, and question my confidence about the trip. I shake that off and focus on accepting where I am at in the journey. Today is a new day, I tell myself. The sun is shining, and the skies are clear. Our team is assembled and I'm in good hands, I decide with a smile. All these changes in our plans have been minor setbacks to be met, measured, and conquered. And we'll start walking after lunch, finally!

As I look out the window, a woman in an orange sari walking with her hand on her companion's arm throws up in the gutter as she walks. She never even stops to wipe her mouth. My smile disappears.

Chapter 8

ON THE MOVE

Besisahar is a popular starting place for the Annapurna Circuit. Driving through the town, we pass under strings of plastic prayer flags that crisscross the streets and are tied to a jumble of electric wires that connect the telephone poles. Open-air stores and businesses that cater to trekkers sit alongside guest houses called Mountain Haven and Majestic View. Metal cisterns catch rainwater on the roofs of the buildings and laundry hangs from the balconies. This is a fascinating but not exactly scenic slice of life in Nepal.

We stop at the Royal Manang Guesthouse and Restaurant for lunch; it's conveniently located around the corner from where we will begin walking. "Royal" is not quite the right word to describe the place; the red wooden tables are sticky, and the red plastic chairs could use a good scrub, but we are closer than ever to getting started and too excited to care. Chuck and I order momos, a type of dumpling popular across

Southeast Asia and the Himalayan region. The mishaps with Bhimsen and Ganesh feel like a natural part of the landscape. No big deal. Ancient history.

Besisahar sits at an elevation of about 2,500 feet. Ram reviews today's plan to walk for four hours along dirt roads and through small lowland villages to a modest 3,000 feet in elevation. The villagers are quick with smiles and greetings of "Namaste," but are too busy preparing for Dashain to be bothered by us. Women gather wood and dung for burning, wearing colorful saris and carrying impossibly heavy baskets strapped to their foreheads. Everywhere they are sweeping, washing, tending to the children, and drying cardamom and millet in the sun.

Dashain honors the Goddess Durga and has a long tradition of animal sacrifice to appease and celebrate the goddess. Three men struggle with a buffalo who stands fast in his tracks and bellows as they tug on the ropes tied around his neck. He seems to have a good idea of what his honored role in the festival will be. Young men herd goats down the path from the higher elevations for the elaborate feasts that will be shared throughout the community.

Farther along, a group of ten men and boys are busy erecting a ping, an oversized community swing made of eight sections of bamboo bent to meet at the top with a considerable amount of tension and fastened with grass-woven ropes. The structure looks like a long-legged spider with a swing hanging from its belly.

"All the villagers take turns on the swing," Ram tells us, "but it's a very big deal for the kids."

The swing looks a little chancy to me, like it might fling an unsuspecting villager should one of its bamboo legs spring loose.

Such an interesting day! We negotiate the first of many suspension bridges we will use to cross the same big river over and back again. Giggling, I give it a pretty good bounce on my way across the wooden slats, some of which are in better shape than others.

After four hours of walking, we reach the village of Ngadi, our stopping place for the night. A few young trekkers are relaxing in a garden filled with a kaleidoscope of flowers—orange marigolds, yellow daisies, and coral-colored cockscomb—along with a few free-ranging chickens pecking at the bugs in the grass. Once again, we are greeted with a cup of masala chai tea, which feels like such a civilized way to end a day's walking. This lodge is perched right on the edge of the big river, and the rooms are a hodgepodge of painted sheds constructed with corrugated steel. I wash a few clothes by hand and hang them on the line in the garden, not confident that they will dry in the humid air before we set out again tomorrow.

Feeling good after our first day of walking, Chuck and I enjoy a dinner of dal bhat and apple fritters. Bhat is rice, and dal are lentils or pigeon peas that are served with a mixture of spicy curried vegetables, sometimes potatoes, sometimes cauliflower, with pickles and greens. Lentils are the most ubiquitous protein available in the mountains.

Our conversation stretches from life in Nepal to Irish politics and music. Chuck tells me about the vibrant music scene in Belfast shaped by jazz, Van Morrison, and U2. He talks about the Irishman's addiction to the "black stuff"—Guinness—and his friends and family back home, especially his grand-daughter, the apple of his eye.

At the end of the evening, I retreat to Shed #9. The bare bulb that hangs from the ceiling doesn't throw off enough light to read, so I take advantage of the last of the daylight to organize my pack, making sure that I can easily reach my roll of toilet paper. There are no western toilets at this lodge, and it is BYOTP. Good thing I did.

I wake up the next morning after a restless sleep. I fell off my wooden platform in the middle of the night, sliding in my sleeping bag right onto the floor. But that wasn't the only thing that woke me up. The raging river is right next to Shed #9, and the clammy night filled my sleep with strange dreams. But I have no complaints. After all, Ram has promised that we will gain considerable elevation today and pass countless waterfalls along the way.

First we need to skirt the edge of the big river—the Marsyangdi—and pass an enormous hydro-electric plant being built to harness its power. The Sinohydro-Sagarmatha Power Company, a Chinese operation, is constructing the facility, investing $150 million in the project. When it comes online in a few years, the power will be shipped back to China to recoup their investment. Eventually, the plant will also supply Nepal's electric grid in hopes of stabilizing the country's chronic power outages. Chinese investment is everywhere, leading to a national debate in Nepal about how natural resources are managed by a sometimes corrupt and inept government.

After the industrial worksite, we begin to climb past terraced rice fields and small villages, many hanging high on mountainsides with steep drops and million-dollar views into the valley. A steady stream of families are on the move, descending from mountain huts to larger villages on the southern slopes of the Annapurna range. These are Gurung people, a tribal sect of the famous Gurkhas. The women wear traditional maroon or red shirts with purple and green skirts and headscarves. They march past waterfalls that cascade alongside the trail, keeping the rice terraces wet and colored vivid shades of lime green. The paddies look like layers of thick velvet stepping their way down the hillside. I snap photo after photo.

After a strenuous day of ascending, we cross an enormously long suspension bridge strung high across the river. The sign says we are leaving the Lamjung District. I don't need a sign to see that we are entering a new and different landscape. Having climbed out of the lowlands and beyond the subtropical climate, the flora turns scrubbier and the path becomes rockier.

Jagat is a stone village catering to trekkers. Ram asks around to see if any of the guest houses offer facilities with a Western toilet, a nod to my preference for a sitting toilet. The more common squat toilet, a hole in the ground with a bucket of water for flushing, is not entirely new to me, but I tend to pee on my shoes if I don't get my stance just right.

Finally, Ram finds a sitting toilet at the Hotel Mont Blanc; never mind that Mont Blanc is a peak in the French Alps and we are in the Himalayas.

An older British couple is resting at a picnic table on the stone terrace. Simon and his wife, Judith, are volunteers in Nepal when they aren't at home in England. He's a farmer and she's a teacher so they decided to bring their professional skills to Nepal for a two-year volunteer assignment, their own post-retirement adventure.

"When we signed up, we knew that we might be temporarily separated," explained Judith. "But we didn't know that we would spend all of our time in Nepal living apart."

Simon continued, "We live with families in villages many miles apart. When the earthquake hit, it took me more than a week before I could get in touch with Judith."

"It was a long week of not knowing if Simon was safe," Judith finished the thought.

"But we were and we're happy to be spending a few weeks of holiday exploring Nepal together," continued Simon.

I marvel at how chill they are.

Chapter 9

BISTARI, BISTARI

Ripping a page out of Simon and Judith's playbook on how to remain stoic and good-humored, I hit my stride today. Plus, I had a flush toilet last night—who needs a seat?—and a decent bed instead of a wooden platform. And, hey, I'm in the middle of a postcard!

A bluebird day starts off cool, but before long I need to shed layers. I stow my down jacket in my daypack and am down to a t-shirt, thanks to the Himalayan sun and the exertion of the climb. With each step, I practice my new vocabulary word—bistari, bistari (slowly, slowly)—my body's only speed as the climb gets steeper. We are on our way to Chame, scrambling up ancient stone steps and down rocky descents with an estimated vertical of more than 2,000 feet. I play a little mind game with myself that I call the Sherpa Shuffle, taking teeny steps in a switchback pattern to trick my body into thinking that I am not walking out of one of the world's deepest gorges, the Kali Gandaki gorge.

The Kali Gandaki gorge, a sheer cut between the Annapurna range and Dhaulagiri massif, has been used as a trading route between India and Tibet for centuries. Spectacular mountain overlooks deliver views into sheer drops, waterfalls, and dramatic rock formations that surround the gorge like an enormous amphitheater.

As we walk higher into the mountains, we begin passing through Buddhist villages. Not only has the geography changed quite noticeably but the religion practiced in these villages has changed from Hinduism to Buddhism. Each village has a series of prayer wheels built into freestanding walls. You can walk on either side of these walls, which are constructed with local stone and topped with Buddhist prayer flags. Even though Ram is a Hindu, he tutors us to pass on the left and use our right hand to spin the wheels for blessings. The wheels are made of metal or wood and are mounted in a long row so that we can run a hand along them as we walk, touching and spinning each one. Many are beautifully embossed and carved with symbols that convey prayers and blessings. I am careful not to knock over the stones that the faithful have left as tokens on ledges and on top of the walls.

These symbols of devotion remind me of the Cruz de Ferro in Spain where I left my own token. At 5,000 feet on the French route of El Camino de Santiago stands a humble metal cross, the Cruz de Ferro. This is the highest point on the pilgrimage and an emotional place for many pilgrims. The ritual is to bring a stone or a memento from home and leave at the base of the cross, leaving with it whatever is troubling you. For me, I was trying to leave behind my worries and insecurities, seeking forgiveness for when I hadn't measured up. Did my Buddhist sisters also kiss their tokens before they tucked them safely into the stony crevices?

The Camino was a transformative journey for me, a rekindling of my Catholic faith. I found enormous inspiration in the Gothic and Romanesque churches of Spain. My own family history was steeped in the religious tenets of Catholicism, so the symbols of God that I saw on the Camino touched my soul in a profoundly spiritual and familiar way. It was many months after going to masses in Spain before I realized that the services had been spoken in a language I didn't understand. And yet I had understood and had been deeply moved.

Here in the mountains of Nepal, I don't find the same spiritual connection. I am fascinated by how people worship differently but I am not awash with the same sense of religious wonder I experienced on the Camino. I am a respectful and curious traveler passing through, not someone of this place.

Chuck and I chat amicably as we walk, asking Ram questions about what we see and telling stories about our lives back home. Chuck grew up as a young man in Belfast during "the Troubles," what the Irish refer to as their civil war between Catholics and Protestants. Chuck lived through a bloody period of Irish history and lost close friends because of the violence.

"There was killing on both sides, all in the name of religion," explains Chuck.

Chuck paints a picture with words when he talks about how civil war ripped his country apart. Considering my own Irish Catholic lineage, I am keenly interested in how religion to this day still divides neighbors and countries.

"I lived through thirty years of a deeply protracted sectarian conflict in my home city of Belfast," he continues. "It's why I consider myself devoutly secular." He had dedicated his career to helping Irish youth find ways to resolve conflicts using civil means to break the cycle of violence.

"I worked with young people in Northern Ireland nurturing leadership skills in a divided society where our main objective was to help them get to know themselves better—their hopes, fears, inhibitions, and emotions. Our approach built their confidence and resilience as they moved on to make their own contribution."

We stop for lunch in the village of Tal and it appears we are the only visitors walking through the town that day. The Potala Guest House advertises a lunch of beans, pumpkin, potato, vegetables, and garlic. The patio of the guesthouse, which is painted red, white, and blue, backs up to a hillside with waterfalls spilling into gullies that flow in the direction of the lake.

"Tal means lake in Nepali," Ram tells us. "Here the river slows, leaving mineral deposits on its banks that look like white sandy beaches."

White sandy beaches in the Himalayas? I am still trying to wrap my head around this comparison as we leave Tal on a path lined with orange and yellow marigolds. Several horses are taking themselves home after a morning of working or grazing, so we step aside to let them continue on their way. They amble by, heads hanging, never giving us a second look. Few people, not even their master, are anywhere to be seen.

The climb out of Tal means crossing the Marsyangdi two more times on suspension bridges that begin to stretch higher and higher over the ice-blue water below. The views are getting bigger and the hanging bridges are getting sturdier; unlike the earlier wooden ones, these are made of steel slats. What had looked like the lazy Marsyangdi just a few hours ago now races and rages in the gorge below us. Ram sets a measured pace, and we stop to catch our breath. Som runs ahead to take photos of us on the bridges with breathtaking drops underneath our feet.

Ram tells us about growing up on a farm in a small village called Bangsing Deurali, two hours west of Pokhara. He learned the basics of English at his village school but became a proficient English speaker as a full-time guide. He has two children and his youngest, a son, is spending Dashain with his grandparents in the family's traditional village. Ram's calm and reassuring demeanor suggests he's seen a lot and has taken all of it in stride.

A small village sits at the top of the hill where we stop for a break. A woman sits cross-legged by a colander of clean apples, tying rope bracelets and anklets. Three young girls smile and watch. Ram catches a praying mantis and lets it walk up this arm as they point and giggle. It's the same delighted reaction that children anywhere would have. I dig into my pack and find the stickers and pens I've tucked away for the children I meet. I think about the money Chuck and I are raising for the school, hoping that the trace we are leaving behind in the Himalayas is a positive one.

As we continue, Ram points out native plants and crops that he can spot from the trail. He forages for walnuts and samples tree fruits like apples and small peaches; occasionally he picks and snacks on what looks like green beans. The altitude is now too high for rice patties and millet, but we pass sparse fields of buckwheat, chickpeas, and beans. Chuck finds wild marijuana growing on the high plateau and I snap an incriminating photo for laughs.

"You could have been a biologist," I tell Ram.

And with that, Ram spots langur monkeys in the hills, their long grey tails curled at the tip like question marks. As quickly as they appear, they are gone.

"How long until we reach the next village?" I ask.

"Two more hours. We should be there by 5," Ram replies.

My heart sinks just a little. The day has already been a strenuous eight hours long. My body is tired from the climb. While Ram doesn't always give me the answer I am hoping for, he is honest and accurate about distances, timetables, and the difficulty of the trail. He does his job so that I can do mine: pace myself and get my head in the right place so that I can mentally prepare for what lies ahead.

Red and white swatches, some spray-painted on rocks, others on trees, are the signposts that trekkers follow on the Annapurna Circuit. Most of the time, though, Chuck and I are simply following Ram. I flash back to the yellow arrows and scallop shells that point the way on the Camino.

The rocky dirt road passes along a fenced-off, restricted area that leads to Tibet, behind it a green expanse of nothing but trees. The border between Tibet and Nepal extends to the east along the Himalayan range, passing through the Everest region and over the highest peak in the world, Mount Everest. While emigration from Tibet to Nepal is forbidden by the Chinese, the traditions and people in this region are heavily influenced by thousands of years of Tibetan migration and cultural cross-pollination.

"Have you ever guided anyone to Everest Base Camp?" I ask Ram.

"I have guided guests to Sagarmatha a few times," he replies.

"Sagarmatha?" I ask Ram to repeat the word.

Mount Everest in Sanskrit, the ancient language of India, is called Sagarmatha, which means forehead of the sky.

"Everest Base Camp is an exciting trek. You must come back, and we will go there together," Ram offers. Everest Base Camp sits at an altitude of 17,600 feet.

Let's survive this one first, I think to myself.

The smell of burning juniper greets us as we walk into Chame, the largest village along the route since setting out from Besisahar. Ram leads us into the common room at the Mona Lisha Teahouse and asks about availability. We have our pick of teahouses: House of Peace and Love, Happy Home Cottage, or Oasis Guest House. I wonder if it shouldn't be the Mona *Lisa* Teahouse. Sometimes the Nepali translations into English are touching in their own wrong way, bringing a smile to my face. The wooden sign hanging out front promises "attached toilet bathroom and gas shower." The promise of a sitting toilet and hot shower seals the deal.

The small common room is crowded at dinner with more people than we have seen, most of whom are not Westerners. As advertised, the Wi-Fi signal is pretty good so I send a few WhatsApp messages to Rick and the kids, telling them that I love them and how we walked in the shadow of Manaslu today, the eighth-highest peak in the world.

Everyone sits as close as possible to a single cast iron stove in the middle of the room and takes turns throwing small logs of wood on the fire. Chuck sits with his back to the stove, letting the heat build along his spine.

"I just can't get warm," he says. This teahouse is situated at the bottom of a particularly narrow section of the valley where both sides shoot up steeply for many thousands of feet. This configuration has the effect of being cold and damp, with little sunlight to dry it out and warm it up each day.

The night has gotten bitterly cold at nearly 9,000 feet, so I get ready for bed by layering up: fleece, hat, tights, and heavy socks, and crawl into my sleeping bag. My rooftop room is windy, and I can smell the stink of the sitting toilet, the reason we booked at the Mona Lisha in the first place. It turns out that sitting toilets don't flush when the temperature drops. Note taken.

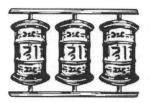

---- Chapter 10 ----

THE GUTS TO GO ON

After a freezing night in a room on the roof of the Mona Lisha, the day dawns with perfect walking temperatures and crystalline blue skies. Either the thinner air or my imagination sharpens the landscape and throws off a full spectrum of colors. Cobalt blue skies reach down to green orchards dotted with red apples. Beyond the grey granite walls that line our walk are the snow-covered peaks of the Annapurna range.

Apples were introduced to the Himalayan foothills after a Nepali man brought Golden and Red Delicious rootstocks back from the Netherlands to experiment with growing them in the local climate. These varietals, and many others planted since that time, thrive on Himalayan hillsides between 8,000 and 9,000 feet. Today, apple orchards have transformed the regional economy, and local farmers depend upon a good apple crop to feed their families and sustain entire villages.

After a morning of hiking, Chuck and I rest on the wooden deck of a small farm overlooking a wall of prayer wheels on a path that winds its way through the apple orchards. Other trekkers are scarce, but the farm is bustling as a gathering place for local workers. A handmade sign is tacked to the wall above wooden bins filled with rosy red apples. It advertises a selection of apple pie, apple fritters, and apple pancakes along with something called apple rum pum.

A little boy plays with his dogs under our picnic table, one of the many beautiful children we meet in the mountains. He must be three or four years old and looks stylish in his blue jeans, white sneakers, and pint-sized jean jacket. His mother has tied a blue scarf around his head to keep his shock of black hair out of his eyes. With outstretched arms, he offers us an apple before racing into the kitchen where his mom is preparing our lunches.

We meet many children in the mountains. I'm not sure if they are not in school because of the festival or if they don't go to school. Friendly and curious, they interact with us through smiles and waves. I dole out the kid-friendly stickers until I run out. Occasionally Ram translates so that we can ask permission to take a photo or give a hug. The children are open to hugs.

Into this idyllic day, a medical reality intrudes. Chuck has come to the Himalayas wearing a heart monitor as a precaution. Several decades ago, he suffered a heart attack and is taking no chances. We talked about this as part of our expedition planning, and Chuck had been fully transparent about tracking his heart rate in an abundance of caution.

A few strides after our lunch break, Chuck draws me aside.

"I feel strange; something has changed."

While we are not on a particularly arduous section of the trail and Chuck is breathing normally, he checks his heart monitor and it reads 170. No sweating or feeling anxious, but a clear reading of 170.

Leaning against a boulder bearing the red and white swatch of the Annapurna Circuit, Chuck tells me that, even though he isn't feeling poorly, he needs to turn back.

"Given my past history with my heart, this is a no-brainer," Chuck says in a calm voice. "As with other mountain emergencies, I have to move back down just as rapidly as possible. We saw two Indian Tata jeeps in Chame that were waiting to journey back down to Besisahar. I should try for a lift on one of them as soon as possible."

I am incredibly fond of my Irish friend and concerned about his health. Chuck looks worried too, but he doesn't appear to be in any physical distress. We both understand the risks of continuing. At the time, Chame was the last village that could be reached by vehicle. If either of us were to experience an emergency higher up in the mountains, we would have to walk back down on our own two feet or, depending upon the nature of the emergency, radio a helicopter to be evacuated.

With a lot of experience in mountaineering and unwilling to risk a medical issue higher up, Chuck makes the decision to end his trek. The four of us turn around and begin a slow, three-hour walk back to Chame where Ram will sort out a jeep for Chuck to return to Besisahar. From there, he will hop a bus back to Pokhara.

I fully support Chuck's decision. We all agree with his plan to return to Pokhara. I know that Chuck is making a decision based upon decades of experience in the mountains, and he knows his own physical condition well enough to know if he needs more urgent medical attention.

I also know that Chuck has my welfare in mind, concerned about how his departure will affect me.

"This trek is a totally new experience for you, well out of your normal comfort zone already," he says. "But I'm confident that you will be well looked after by Ram should you decide to continue," he adds. "This is your decision."

As we descend, I sort through my own feelings. Once again, I am at a pivot point. I work hard to tamp down that terrible gnawing worry that makes me fear the worst. Should I return to Besisahar and Pokhara with Chuck or do I press on with Ram and Som? My body is feeling pretty strong, although we are still at only 9,000 feet in altitude. With a guide and a porter, I wouldn't be alone in the Himalayas. Have I come all this way to turn back now?

Once again, I ask myself, "Okay, Tracy, now what are you going to do?"

When your plans have been derailed—and this goes for anything—it becomes a test of how resilient you are moving forward. We all have times when things go sideways. As I take stock of my feelings, I feel like I've got this. In fact, once I get out of my head, I decide that the part of the journey that hasn't terrified me has been quite enjoyable. Despite all the setbacks we have encountered so far, I now know what to expect.

I begin a little conversation with myself.

"Okay, Tracy, which way are you going to go? Up or down?"

I run down a checklist of questions.

"Should I return to Pokhara with Chuck?"

Chuck is insistent that there is no need for all of us to turn back with him. In fact, he has made a good case for me to continue.

I check in with my body.

"No aches. No blisters. Tired each day but fit enough," I tell myself. Check.

"What about your personal safety, Tracy?"

"You're safe and not in any danger," I reply. Big check.

"Are you up for the challenge?" I ask myself.

"You came because of the challenge," I coach myself.

I scan my emotional state, which could be the roadblock to moving forward. While my body has been strong enough, my resolve has certainly been strained. I'm not feeling at the peak of confidence and courage, but I decide that my emotional endurance passes muster too.

"If you quit overwhelming yourself with worry and lighten up, you can do this."

I think of a dear friend describing worrying as "praying for what you don't want."

"What are you so afraid of?"

"I guess I'm afraid that I can't do it." Well, there is only one way to find out.

And so I rock from the back of my heels to the balls of my feet and lean into the adventure.

With Chuck's encouragement, I decide to continue my trek on the Annapurna Circuit as far as Manang. This is an ancient trading post and resting place for trekkers who use it to acclimatize before crossing the Thorung La pass. Since I am wracked with worry about crossing the high pass, I decide to walk to Manang and turn around there. At the end of what I expect to be another eight days, I too will make the trek-jeep-bus trip back to Pokhara and meet back up with Chuck.

As is so often the case with travelers whose paths cross and then diverge, we go our separate ways, each on our own journeys, until we will meet up again.

So I find the guts to go on. After several hours—first retracing our steps through the orchards and then continuing past Swargadwari Danda, Heaven's Door, where locals believe souls climb up to the heavens—we walk along a ledge cut into the side of the gorge, which now consists of sheer vertical walls of granite rising 4,000 feet around us. Eventually we reach a forest filled with pine trees and the autumn colors of the Himalayas. I spy my first yak grazing on the scrub. Yaks here are used as beasts of burden but are also prized for their milk, cheese, and meat. Seeing these native animals framed by the Himalayas punctuates how foreign the landscape feels.

The next day we reach the wooden village of Upper Pisang crawling up the side of the mountain at 11,000 feet. Primitive buildings are connected by rickety staircases that zig and zag their way to rooms stacked on different levels. My accommodation at the Tibet Guest House consists of a single platform covered in a hard, thin mattress and a blanket. The kitchen is bustling as I place my dinner order of dal bhat and request a bucket of boiling hot water for washing up. I haven't washed my clothes or myself for several days, although I'm not sure anyone cares. Still, it is a good time to make an effort.

Finally sorted and ready for dinner, I head to the common room, the only room that is heated. Ram sits on the floor at a single low table looking at a map. Faded family photos, dated calendars of summer scenes in the Himalayas, and postcards from around the world are thumbtacked to the walls, but it's the big view outside the windows that catches my eye. Annapurna II, at more than 26,000 feet and one of the highest peaks in the world, rises across the valley right in front of me.

The view is shocking by its very enormity. Annapurna II is unobstructed, her grandeur lording over the peaks around her and a gray glacier at her base that looks as hard as concrete. I can see the big river, tossed like a girl's opalescent hair ribbon, on the dusty valley floor.

A smattering of 20-something trekkers are chatting and looking at photos and maps. Two young British women have been taking a holiday on the circuit after a two-month teaching assignment in India. A Russian trekker named Oleg keeps mostly to himself until the room empties and we all head for the Buddhist temple, called a gompa, located at the top of the hill.

I climb the stone steps and am greeted by a stuffed condor stretched out above the doorway of the monks' quarters. The condor is called the "king of the sky" because of its enormous size and ten-foot wingspan. It peers down on me with beady eyes like I am dinner. I wonder if it hangs there to ward off evil spirits.

As if on cue, a monk wearing Crocs ducks through the doorway and leads us wordlessly into Pisang's Buddhist temple, his saffron-colored robe whipping in the wind.

The temple is guarded by a once-fearsome deity carved out of wood. But its wild eyes, long fangs, and sharp claws are now faded and weathered by the harsh Himalayan elements. Inside the gompa, the pungent aroma of burning juniper fills the room with smoke, catching in my throat. A few visitors in down jackets and hiking boots wander around a single ornate room with a slightly raised dais along one wall and a Buddhist shrine of candles and photos along another. Every inch of the interior—walls, ceiling, and columns—is artfully painted with geometric shapes and colors. A lion, its paw raised, takes up an entire wall next to an altar filled with offerings of apples, faded fake flowers, and photos of the Dalai Lama.

The bang of a gong signals that the Buddhist prayer ceremony is about to begin. I find a cushion and sit on the floor facing six monks who chant themselves into a trance-like state. One monk rings a bell, another alternates between banging a gong and pair of cymbals. But the main attractions for me are the prayer horns, hollowed out from the horns of a yak or an ox, that wail a haunting call as part of the ceremony.

After twenty minutes, the monks are finished, and I get up from my cushion. A single star in the sky is rising over Annapurna II as we troop back down the hillside to the Tibet Guest House. I am feeling a long way from home, no doubt about it.

I wake up the next morning with ice in my veins and a throbbing headache, thanks to the altitude. Even the Russian trekker, Oleg, remarks how bitterly cold it is. I meet Ram and Som in the breakfast room, my gear ready to go.

"We will be taking the high road from Upper Pisang to Nawal," says Ram. "It is harder, but the high road is the scenic route," he promises.

We move slowly, climbing above 12,000 feet through pine forests and past stalls abandoned by their owners. They stand waiting for better days, when they will once again sell souvenirs to a parade of trekkers. Mount Pisang peers out of the woods. She is not nearly as high as the Annapurnas, but her conical white hat is memorable as she gazes over the next village of Ghyaru. A manmade whirl catches our attention, and we watch a helicopter speed toward the village.

"What's happening?" I ask Ram as we walk toward thirty people who are waiting for the helicopter to land.

Ram speaks to one of the men. "They are taking a local man who is very sick to a hospital in Kathmandu."

The entire village watches as the man is carried on a stretcher to the heli.

"How can this man from a poor mountain village afford an airlift to Kathmandu?"

"It is possible that the whole village contributed several thousand dollars to pay for his transport," replies Ram as we watch the expensive ambulance lift off.

---- Chapter 11 ----

MARION'S TAVERN

"We will have a hard day today. We are headed up," Ram says as he points up and over the trees.

As I follow the upward line of his finger, I squint to barely make out a hint of colors flapping in the wind. Our destination seems extremely far away. It's so steep that I wonder how I will ever get there. The altitude is now making every single step hard-fought, so I use the Sherpa Shuffle and concentrate on what I am doing. All my focus is on the here and now.

We take a break at the first and only manned stall we come across, "manned" by two beautiful young women who are selling an assortment of snacks, and Cokes. I buy three Snickers bars, and we stow them in our packs. Looking back at the path, I marvel that we are actually making progress, crawling up the mountain at a snail's pace.

It's now been several days since Chuck turned back. With every confidence that he returned safely to Pokhara, I still worry about his health. I had looked forward to the solitude after we parted and the opportunity to be alone with my thoughts in the Himalayas. But I am struggling as much with loneliness as with the physical strain. My walk on El Camino de Santiago, in contrast, was a social experience. I enjoyed meeting countless pilgrims from all over the world and even making several lifelong friends. Ram and Som are kind and capable men, but the cultural and language barrier precludes us from the same kind of companionship that I experienced on the Camino. That lack of community and common ground leaves me feeling empty and very alone in the Himalayas, even though I am accompanied.

Finally, we approach the last stretch to reach the crest of the hill. The switchbacks are now carved into the side of the mountain and not just in my mind. At the top, I can see a few people resting and taking photos of the big view just beyond. The color I had glimpsed from below are prayer flags lashed to a pole wedged at the end of a long, tapered ledge. The ledge juts out over nothing but air. I take a deep breath and work up the nerve to inch out onto the narrow ledge and glue myself to the pole as the flags whip around me. Once again, I have an unobstructed view of the Annapurna massif with a faraway blue glimmer of the Marsyangdi snaking her way along the valley floor. I am hanging on tight as I find Tree Pose, a balanced yoga pose, while never letting go of the wooden pole.

At this moment, life is in full relief. The sun is brilliant, and I forget my lingering headache as I stand surrounded by the glorious Himalayas. Billy goats bleat on the ledge just below me. A local boy in a faded and tattered sweater smiles broadly under his hooded sweatshirt. I'm not sure where his family is as he wanders among the trekkers, including a middle-aged couple who are smiling at him.

Once my knees stop shaking from peering over the ledge, I make my way over to this tall and handsome couple to say hello.

"Namaste!" I smile.

"Namaste and hi!" I have heard this accented English before.

"We're Bob and Elly from the Netherlands. We're Dutch," continues Bob.

My grocery store chain in the U.S. was owned by a Dutch company, so over the course of a decade, I made more than a dozen visits to the Netherlands. I got to know and love the country and especially the Dutch. One November, I worked for three weeks on a special assignment in the corporate headquarters in Amsterdam. My Camino bestie, a woman with whom I walked much of El Camino de Santiago, is Dutch, and everywhere I have traveled off the beaten path, I have met Dutch people continuing a centuries-old tradition of exploration.

Bob and Elly are friendly and easygoing. They live and work in Utrecht but are in Nepal for humanitarian work and a sidebar trek on the Annapurna Circuit. Elly is a podiatrist who takes several weeks each year to provide foot care at a Nepalese school near the capital. Bob is a landscape architect and, as we walk together for the rest of the day, he tells me about the garden boxes he built for the students to grow their own vegetables.

Hungry for conversation and companionship, I am happy when the three of us end up at the Hotel Peaceful in Nawal, an establishment run by a local woman and her husband, a retired Nepali policeman. Since I haven't been able to shake my altitude-induced headache, they serve me garlic soup and ginger-lemon tea, a local remedy. Between that and a steady diet of ibuprofen, I am feeling better by dinnertime, able to enjoy a newly minted friendship.

"I've been looking for a luxury hotel with a heated swimming pool to soak my feet," Bob tells me over dinner. "Have you found a hotel with a swimming pool yet?" A sly grin spreads across his face.

"I hear there are hot springs in Tatopani," I tell him, on to the joke. "If you survive the high pass, you can soak your tired feet there. As for the luxury hotel, perhaps you have chosen the wrong place."

We laugh all evening as he continues his running joke about sitting poolside at a fancy hotel.

My final outbound destination of Manang is in the crosshairs the next day. But first there is a short and relatively level walk to one of the oldest Buddhist monasteries in the Himalayas.

The Braga monastery hangs off a hillside overlooking a flat, dry plateau in the rain shadow of the Annapurna range. Horses and yaks graze along the river with a new peak in view, Gangapurna, her glacier sliding down the mountain into a milky blue lake. The sky sports a deeper hue of turquoise in thinner air; we are now above the tree line but still below the snow line.

Elly and Bob and a young Italian couple have joined us. We climb the worn stone steps and try the door of the monastery, which is locked. The Italians seem to know the drill and go looking for the caretaker. They return with an ancient and very stooped man who agrees to open the door for 100 rupees. We leave our shoes at the entrance and wander past colorful wooden carvings and countless statues of Buddha. One wall is filled with the same sitting Buddha in row after row, three deep. The dim light casts eerie shadows on fierce wooden masks and shrines crowded with photos of a smiling Dalai Lama. Faces seem to be looking at me from everywhere.

THE FACES AT BRAGA (EXCERPT)

By David Whyte; Reprinted with permission

In monastery darkness
by the light of one flashlight,
the old shrine room waits in silence.

While above the door
we see the terrible figure,
fierce eyes demanding, 'Will you step through?'

And the old monk leads us,
bent back nudging blackness,
prayer beads in the hand that beckons.

We light the butter lamps
and bow, eyes blinking in the
pungent smoke, look up without a word,

see faces in meditation,
a hundred faces carved above,
eye lines wrinkled in the hand-held light.

Such love in solid wood. Taken from the hillsides
and carved in silence, they have
the vibrant stillness of those who made them.

Engulfed by the past
they have been neglected, but through
smoke and darkness they are like the flowers

we have seen growing
through the dust of eroded slopes,
their slowly opening faces turned toward the mountain.

The roof of the monastery offers the best view for photos. The village of Manang is situated several kilometers up the path and I stop just short of congratulating myself for accomplishing what I said I would do. Manang will be a good turning-around point, I tell myself. It's an exotic and memorable place, part of a centuries-old network of trading routes that connected China, India, and Tibet with Central Asia.

Manang is also the last stop before crossing Thorung La and the gateway to one of the most isolated places in the world, the Mustang district of Nepal. Few destinations in the world feel so untouched. On the edge of the Tibetan plateau, the Mustang landscape features cliffs and caves and gompas famous for how hard they are to reach. The inaccessibility of this remote corner of the world has helped it to preserve its Tibetan culture and Buddhist ways. Manang, still on this side of the pass, feels like the end of the world to me, with nothing but an ancient and unfamiliar land in the reaches just beyond.

* * * * *

Remember Marion's tavern in *Raiders of the Lost Ark*? Called The Raven, the local watering hole was located in the rugged and faraway mountains of Nepal where a motley assortment of patrons wagered on whether they could drink Marion under the table.

With visions of The Raven in my head, I wonder, "Where are you, Indy?"

There is no Raven or Marion's tavern in Manang, so we check into the Hotel New Yak, specializing in yak steak, yak burgers, yak cheese toasties, and yak milk, according to the sign. I am game for anything other than dal baht.

The guides gather at wooden tables in an anteroom while guests are seated in a larger room for tea and meals. There are a few middle-aged European men with their sons and nephews who look ready to tackle the high pass after a day of rest and acclimatization. There is an element of excitement in the air and a great deal of testosterone in the room. Elly and I are the only women there.

I make plans to meet Elly and Bob for dinner and a movie. Yes, there is a primitive movie theater here in Manang. But first, Ram and Som and I have a job to do.

Chuck had given me the Tibetan prayer flags we purchased in Kathmandu to hang in triumph for both of us at 18,000 feet.

Since I have decided not to cross Thorung La, Ram suggests that we hike to Gangapurna Lake and hang the prayer flags there. Gangapurna's glacial lake spreads out below an enormous icefall that overlooks the village. Ram scrambles over the fence and begins tying the green flag to the highest point he can reach.

"Be careful!" I call out as the wind whips and pulls at the flags. Ram is standing in a precarious spot with loose rocks under his feet and a freefall down into the lake.

I hold tightly onto the other end and stretch the flags towards a gatepost for fastening. Som and I work on one side of the fence while Ram finishes his work. Karma Sherpa told us that it's important to think a good thought when hanging the prayer flags. My thoughts turn to gratitude. I say my own kind of prayer, thankful that I made it to this special place and can now get back to my family. Sometimes adventure travel takes us so far away that we just need to go home.

I remember back to the monk who blessed the flags and wonder if he threw a few detours into my journey to test my resolve. If so, he certainly succeeded.

On our way back into the village, I look back at the Gangapurna icefall. Strings of flags flap in the wind above the glacier; ours are easy to pick out, still new and brightly colored. It won't be long until they fade and tatter like the others. I wave goodbye to Ram and Som and head to the movie theater to meet Bob and Elly.

The Annapurna High Vision Hall is a small concrete block building with a white door and rocks on the roof to keep the wind from blowing it off. Elly, Bob, and I pay $2.50 at the door and are treated to the Manang version of movie concessions, a small bag of popcorn and a cup of black tea. Twenty wooden benches are lined up and, since we are the only ones in the theater, we test out a few spots before settling in with our parkas and popcorn.

Outside, a crude sign advertises the rotation of five movies, a relevant but chilling selection of titles considering our location.

> *Into Thin Air*
> *Seven Years in Tibet*
> *Into the Wild*
> *Caravan Himalaya*
> *Touching the Void*

When we talk about what movie we want to see, Elly votes for *Into Thin Air*. "*Into Thin Air?*" I double-check. This movie is at the bottom of my list.

"*Into Thin Air* might not be the best movie to see before crossing the high pass," I suggest. "You do know that this movie is about a disaster in these, *these* very mountains?"

Journalist and climber Jon Krakauker won numerous literary awards for his true story about an expedition gone wrong on Mount Everest. In May 1996, a gathering storm, combined with poor decisions, turned an attempt to summit the world's tallest mountain into a gruesome tale of death and dying. The movie does a great job putting you right there, as if I weren't close enough to begin with.

In case I am not getting my point across, I add, "It's about people dying in the Himalayas."

I know that we are not climbing Mount Everest like the expedition in the movie, but we are only one big valley away. While I am not keen on seeing *Into Thin Air* again, I'm more wigged out about Elly and Bob watching it just hours before crossing Thorung La.

"It will be fine," Elly reassures me.

Not wanting to spoil our last evening together, I smile weakly and sip my tea.

Thirty minutes into the movie, I'm done with it. I thought I could watch the entire movie but ask myself, "Why would you want to do that?" so I whisper goodbye and sneak back into the evening.

The sky is still light, so I wander through the tourist section of town and toward the old stone village where the locals live. The path narrows and there are no longer teahouses or bakeries with German apple strudel on display in their windows. Flat-roofed stone houses are surrounded by a warren of alleyways that can be navigated only on foot. I don't venture into the alleyways and invade what feels like private property. The main path leads directly in front of Gangapurna and Mount Tilicho. The sun has dropped behind the mountains, so I turn back as it gets dark. A rustic souvenir shop catches my eye and I dig through an assortment of warm Nepali hats before purchasing just the right one, a blue and green knit hat with a tassel on top and woven ties, like braided pigtails, hanging down the sides.

Outside the Hotel New Yak, I meet Elly and Bob, who also bailed on the movie when the climbers began dying.

"Perhaps you were right!" Elly says cheerfully. My Dutch friends do not have disaster on their minds, but they didn't need to finish out the death and dying scenes either.

"Tomorrow, we are headed over the high pass and the weather looks good!" Elly says. I am so impressed with their fortitude and sense of adventure.

"I am headed back down the mountain tomorrow but not before I take a pony ride."

I had decided that, before leaving Manang I would treat myself to a pony ride. Ram said he would talk to the vendors offering pony porters and line up a short ride for me the next morning.

I say my goodbyes to Elly and Bob at breakfast. Then, like a little girl, I am tickled pink to ride a pony named Kala in the Himalayas. I sit on several rough blankets and hold onto a heavy rope for the reins. Kala reminds me of the Chincoteague ponies from home, sturdy and strong, just like me. Kala is my reward for doing what I promised myself I would do.

Ram and Som run ahead and take photos, making sure that we pose at every turn and don't miss the money shots in front of Gangapurna and Mount Tilicho. While it is a very tame ride, the world looks a little different from a saddle. After all, the horse does all the work, giving me a chance to catch my breath and look up instead of down.

I take mental snaps and think about how I got here. Now that I have reached my turnaround point, I should feel a sense of accomplishment, even victory. This trek has been hard on me, not what I expected, and I have struggled to stay glued together. But I made it to Manang and I feel more like a survivor, one with a better sense of her limitations than she had a few weeks ago.

After the three of us take turns riding Kala, we set out for the six-hour walk to Dhikur Pokhari. The wind kicks up and the weather changes as we walk into valleys hidden from the sunlight.

Chapter 12

THE MOST DANGEROUS ROAD IN THE WORLD

I pull my bandana over my mouth and nose to keep from eating the dust and turn to walk down the mountain. While I am happy to be moving to lower ground, I still have several days of walking ahead, and my reserve of emotional energy is depleted. I got my pony ride when I made it to Manang, just as I said I would. Maybe it's just the wind in my eyes but I have a little cry, feeling very far from home and pining for somewhere warm and clean.

We are making our way to the night's resting place in Dhikur Pokhari. We didn't pass through this village and are taking a new route on the way down. There are a few villages along the way, and every one of them is a ghost town. Today is the most important day of the festival, so we see almost no one.

The Kamala Hotel in Dhikur Pokhari is painted an incongruous but colorful mix of teal, lavender, and pink. The tables on the terrace along the road are empty, just like the tables at the teahouse across the street. A sign above the free-standing arch promises 24 hours of electricity, a hot shower, and good food.

The suggestion of good food means more dal bhat. Except for a slightly overcooked yak burger in Manang, I have now eaten lentils and beans for ten straight days. The three of us sit alone in the main room of the teahouse, which also serves as the restaurant. Ram and Som mix small portions of rice together with the dal and curry, using only their right hands. A spoon is always available in the teahouses for me and, when he is feeling western, Som uses a utensil as well.

These two men have been kind and companionable to me, even if the conversation has been limited. Once Chuck turned back, the two days I spent in the company of Elly and Bob were the closest I got to an easy conversation, one that came from a shared western outlook. That common ground can't be underestimated.

We take much for granted and then, when we are thrown into something entirely different, with people who have a different cultural point of view, it's hard. Everyone is polite. Conversations are brief and fact-based. The limitations that surface in this kind of cultural immersion can be exhausting. To say that I am tired and ready to be done would be an under-statement. But I accept the fact that I will have to carry on for a few more days.

Since there is no wood in sight Ram asks the owners to throw a few more logs on the fire to warm up the room. Despite sitting close, the heat thrown off from the stove isn't enough to keep us warm. I'm so cold I decide to go to bed.

I can see my breath when I wake up—inside. I slept in my parka and new knit hat, and I'm still wearing my headlamp from my midnight bio break. I congratulate myself for not falling down the shaky staircase on my way to a squatting toilet at the far edge of the patio below.

Typically, there are two buckets in the toilet area, one for dirty TP and the other for flushing and washing up the floor, should that be required. I use a nearby spigot to fill up my red bucket for flushing, trying hard not to splash my feet. Toilet etiquette aside, they say that the squat holes in the ground are more sanitary and possibly healthier than sitting toilets. As we climbed higher, sitting toilets all but disappeared. Or at least none are advertised on the teahouse signs.

Ram's job today is to get us to Chame and hire a jeep for the journey down the mountain to Besisahar. Jeeps are scarce and the first few we see are filled beyond what you might think is humanly possible. A gnawing desperation settles into my belly, a similar sensation to a day-long hunger. Even though we are on the way down, I find this part of the journey hard on me emotionally. My goal is no longer to reach my turnaround point, at which time I could say, "I did it." I got there and I'm still not finished. *I'm still not finished.*

We pass a small airstrip, which I later learn is used only in perfect weather conditions. I also learn that even in the best of conditions, landing between these Himalayan peaks is a thrill ride. Every pilot has to be an expert in short takeoffs and landings.

"An airport!" I exclaim with real surprise. "You didn't tell me we could fly."

I would pay a small ransom to catch a flight, but the winds are whipping. I search the airstrip and see no planes.

"Flying to Pokhara is not an option," Ram assures me. He can't see the tears welling up in the back of my eyes. I would've paid any price to speed up the ten-hour jeep ride back to Besisahar.

Two small children are resting on the rocks, taking a break from hauling their enormous bundles of sticks. Children learn early how to forage and haul heavy baskets on their backs, secured by a strap around their foreheads. We are all smiles, surprised to come upon each other in the middle of the mountains. I search my pockets and mentally unpack my bag. I've given away all of my stickers and token gifts. Do I have any chocolate? I hand the children the one apple I have stowed in my pack and ask Ram to see if they will pose with me for a photo. Like many of the Nepali children I meet in the mountains, they smile until the camera comes out, at which time they pose with straight faces.

Afterwards they giggle and I hug them both for an extra-long moment. "Namaste," we call out in fare-well.

* * * * *

When we arrive in Chame, Ram begins asking around for a jeep, and eventually we get lucky and hire a relatively empty one for the ride to Besisahar. The price is steep, and I must pay for not only my transport but also the fares for Ram and Som. Ram tells me that my rate is higher since I am a foreigner. My charge is 40,000 rupees; Ram and Som are 2,000 rupees each. The exchange rate is roughly one dollar to 100 Nepali rupees, so the total of 44,000 rupees or $440 is all the cash I have left. But the alternative, walking for another four days, is out of the question. I don't have another four days of walking in me, not physically, not emotionally. Out of money? I will figure that out down below.

Beginning in 2010, a single jeep track was chiseled out of the rockface on what is popularly referred to as the most dangerous road in the world. During the rainy season on the Besisahar-Chame road, gigantic waterfalls pour onto the road, covering it with running water and making travel riskier than ever.

Ram insists that I sit near the "inside" window of the jeep on our ten-hour drive down the most dangerous road in the world so I won't be able to see how close we get to the vertical drops that freefall into the Marsyangdi River below. To perish now, two days after finishing a physically arduous and emotionally draining trek on the Annapurna Circuit, would be a shame.

Our driver, who looks 12 years old, maneuvers the jeep like a seasoned pro, hugging the edge of the narrow track, past the potholes and through the waterfalls gushing onto the road and down the other side. He is dressed like a teenager with dark jeans and sandals, a dark blue sweatshirt with stars and a base-ball cap to match, worn backwards, of course. He wears a cheerful smile and a windbreaker the same shade of purple as mine.

The driver picks up more and more passengers on the way down. A remarkable eighteen people squeeze into the jeep, including eight of us in the cab and a little boy who sleeps wedged comfortably between the driver and another passenger. The little boy has been handed through the window by his mother before she climbs into the back, where Ram and Som are bouncing around with the packs. A young man stands on the floorboard of the jeep and hops off to remove rocks the size of watermelons when they block the way. I wonder if loading more people in the cargo bed reduces the amount of jostling on the bumpy road.

Descending the narrow track, we pass porter after porter carrying loads that look to be several times their body weight. Squeezed in cheek by jowl, I wince as the door handle delivers another punch to my hip. As I peer out the window, I am astonished to see a group of five mountain bikers kitted out in western bicycle clothes who are stopped and panting hard as they press against the steep inside wall. One man appears to be weeping with his head bent into the crook of his arm. After the pounding journey I've just been through, I understand his pain. These mountains make grown men cry.

My jeep mates settle in for a long but companionable ride. Most of them are leaving the mountains after visiting their families for the festival. A group of twenty-something friends from Kathmandu are returning from a hike to Tilicho Lake, the highest lake in the world. They show me their photos and called me Didi, an affectionate term that means older sister. When we stop to look at the waterfalls, they invite me to pose with them for their photos. They are handsome and outgoing.

Hindi pop music blares the whole way, and the boys in the cab sing along to their favorite tunes. The young men are affectionate with each other, and many times I have noticed Nepali men hugging or walking with their arms linked. The Nepali people have a genuine friendliness, both with foreigners and with each other. It's as if life is hard enough, so kindness and compassion are a common standard. They show a deep reverence for their elders; they look you in the eye and give a ready smile, and they have a wonderful curiosity that compels them to ask, "Where you from?"

I am a bit bruised by the time we reach Besisahar and everyone pours out of the jeep. It reminds me of a clown car spitting out an improbable number of passengers.

Ram calls out for me to pay the driver our agreed-upon price while he and Som unload the packs. We are parked in front of an open-air café, a bare bulb casting a weak light on a few tables with patrons. My young driver and I go to a table to count out my rupees. Since I have only 100- and 50-rupee notes, I count out more than 44 bills. People gather to watch.

My driver grins a big boyish smile as I hand him the wad of money and say, "Now you count it." I'm wondering if he understands English when our transaction is suddenly interrupted by a wide-eyed Ram.

Running to the table, he shouts, "What are you doing?"

"I'm paying the man." It's been a long day and I'm a little confused. Isn't this my job?

"The price is 8,000 rupees—4,000 for you and 2,000 each for Som and me!"

Having somehow heard 40,000 rupees for me, I have just handed over a king's ransom with all Besisahar watching.

I gently reach across the table, eyes locked with my driver, and pull the wad of cash back. After I count out 8,000 rupees, I start breathing again. In any other country, this moment might have led to a stick-up or an ambush. In Nepal, $440 is enough money to sustain a family for a year.

I go off in search of a drink and a cigarette.

Although I had clearly heard Ram wrong about the tourist price, I think to myself, "What a rookie mistake." One of the challenges of traveling alone— or at least making every decision yourself—is that you don't have anyone else to discuss things with. No one with whom to problem solve and commiserate with when issues arise. No one to help you when, in sheer exhaustion, you get it wrong.

I shake my head in disgust as I walk to a small kiosk to buy an Everest beer and a ten-pack of smokes. I figure that since the last few days hadn't killed me, a few Marlboros won't either. Now that I am at a lower altitude, I don't worry as much about gasping for air at 18,000 feet.

As I sit on a plastic chair outside of my night's lodging, I say a little prayer to sleep through the night and arrive back in Pokhara the next day without losing my shirt. Running low on both money and courage, I can't afford any more mistakes.

Chapter 13

TYPE II FUN

Our fully-loaded bus dances its way from Besisahar to Pokhara, bumping and grinding to a lunchtime stop at the Nepali version of a roadside restaurant. Many passengers find a clean patch of ground to eat their packed lunches, or they take a walk to stretch their legs. I am desperate for a bathroom, so I head to the edge of the parking lot where three squat holes are lined up like outhouses behind individual wooden doors.

After a short wait, I'm ready to take my turn.

I look inside and look again in disbelief.

"Whoa!"

The ground is covered in excrement, with no clean place to put my feet. Used toilet paper litters the inside edges of the outhouse walls. I turn on my heels and take a walk of my own, looking for privacy away from the busy road, much of my modesty forgotten somewhere in the Himalayas.

When we pull into Pokhara a few hours later, I get a little choked up as I say goodbye to Ram and Som.

We exchange information to stay in touch and Som offers to show me the sights in Pokhara from the back of his motorbike before I leave.

"Good-bye, Som; thank you for carrying my big bag. And thank you for taking pictures of me that I will remember forever." I give him a big smile as our handshake turns into a hug.

Turning to Ram, I shake my trusted guide's hand. "Ram, you have been a wonderful guide. Thank you for everything."

"You must come to my home," Ram offers with a sweet smile. It's both a question and an invitation. I thank him again and tell him that I will let him know, unsure of my plans for the next few days.

I am not so emotionally drained that I don't appreciate the esprit de corps I shared with my two walking companions, two men supporting their families by leading travelers into the Himalayas. They have to be ready to handle any set of circumstances in the mountains, from unpredictable weather to clients who get sick, maybe even with AMS, to other dangerous conditions like mudslides. They also need to manage the needs of many types of guests: the demanding ones, complaining types, and know-it-alls. I have tried to be a good guest myself and, in return, Ram and Som have provided me with equal parts of safety, camaraderie, and encouragement.

Despite what feels like friendship, I don't forget that these two men are working. I hand over most of my remaining rupees and tip them generously, saving just what I estimate I might need before heading home.

Back at the Hotel Tulsi, Chuck and I greet each other enthusiastically. I haven't seen anyone I know for more than a week, and it's good to see a familiar smile in a country so far from home. Chuck is eager to hear about the rest of the trek.

I give him the shorthand version and show him photos of the Gangapurna Icefall where I hung our Buddhist prayer flags. I ask him how he is feeling.

"I've been feeling fine, just sitting around, really. No signs of heart stress. As much as I love Pokhara, I've seen what there is to see here, so I've booked a three-day trek to Poon Hill," he tells me. "I leave tomorrow."

Poon Hill is a relatively short but spectacular trek to just under 10,000 feet. For a walk classified as easy to moderate, the payoff is big. Many trekkers plan their journey to reach the crest of Poon Hill at dawn for views of Dhaulagiri, Machapuchare, and Annapurna II illuminated by the sunrise.

"Oh." I fight hard to process this information.

I've been on my own for eight days and have another four days until my return flight home from Kathmandu. I'm pissed but I feel I really shouldn't be. Chuck has been cooling his heels for more than a week and is anxious to salvage his trip. Nepal is a long way from Belfast and who knows when he will return. Frankly, if I were Chuck, I might do the same. While I wish he had trekked to Poon Hill while I was in the mountains, I understand the reasons behind his decision.

For me, this final shift in plans seems like a fitting ending to the saga filled with twists and turns.

As friends who have shared a number of adventures and misadventures on this trip, traveling at times on the same and then on separate paths, Chuck and I muddle through an awkward meal that evening, wish each other well, and say goodbye.

On my own again the next day, I walk down the main drag until I find what I am looking for: a small tourist agency. Behind the desk is an earnest young man who introduces himself as Shiva.

"Hello, Shiva. I would like to change my flights back to the U.S.," I tell him. "Do you think you can help me?"

For the next three hours, Shiva works the phone and his computer, but it's hard to get through. At one point, he calls his cousin who lives near the airport in Kathmandu and asks him to visit the Qatar Air desk personally. While I wait, Shiva serves me cup after cup of masala chai tea and apologizes for the delay.

"Shiva," I say, "If you can rebook my flights, I will wait as long as I have to." The Wi-Fi is good in the tourist agency, and I turn back to checking in with Rick, keeping him posted on my plans.

Finally, Shiva is able to move up my return trip home by two days. That gives me one more day to look around Pokhara before I catch two long flights back to Philadelphia. I thank Shiva profusely and head out into the day.

I spend my last day in Pokhara writing and reflecting, looking forward to my final dinner at Ram's house. I hire a rowboat for a ride across Phewa Lake. For $5, a man rows me across the lake and, with bits of English and lots of smiling, he points out the rhesus monkeys scrambling through the trees on the other side. Families have hired boats and are making a pilgrimage to the Hindu temple in the middle of the lake as part of their festival celebrations. Back on the shore, vendors are selling colorful balloons, plush toys, and fake flowers for offerings at the island temple. A wooden Ferris wheel with four rough-hewn benches circles slowly, its seats filled with giggling kids and teens.

Along the way, I say my goodbyes to Nepal. As I contemplate Phewa Lake with her big mountains keeping watch from a distance, I am overwhelmed with relief that I am finally headed home.

As I take stock of the trip, I have a deep sense of gratitude that I've been given an opportunity to experience this landscape and its people, which has been eye-opening from a cultural perspective and provided a window into the lives of people living close to the edge of survival. Walking through these mountain villages in the year of destruction gave me a close look at the hardships that they face with remarkable resilience.

Traveling in the developing world is hard work, but it's not as hard as living here. The last three weeks have given me the chance to learn firsthand about the beauty and adversity at the top of the world and see how people live here. What do they do? How do they love? What are their hopes and dreams? Many of these people dream of living the life we live in America, reminding me of my own blessings and the freedom to move around the globe.

As a final farewell, Ram has invited me to his home for a family dinner of dal bhat with his wife and 17-year-old daughter. I feel honored and try to be a gracious guest, leaving my shoes at the door. Ram's wife smiles shyly when I present her with a small bouquet of flowers—real ones, not the plastic offering kind. Although she doesn't speak English, Ram and his daughter are happy to translate. Before I leave, I hand Ram my Steripen.

"Thank you, Ram, for taking such good care of me," I tell him with great sincerity. I figure that this gizmo to purify water will be of more use to Ram than to me. He accepts my gift with a small bow, and I say goodbye to the one person who has been my trusted shepherd for the duration of the walk. I feel very

lucky to have had him and his gentle demeanor leading the way.

The next day, I arrive early at the Pokhara Airport
to begin my long slog home. Shiva had had no choice
but to book me a flight with a seven-hour layover in
Kathmandu. That's okay with me since I have
nowhere else to go. Chuck tipped me off that Qatar
Air has a comfortable private lounge, so I follow the
signs and talk my way in, even though I am not a
preferred customer with the airline.

"I'm sorry, Ma'am, but this lounge is reserved for
our Privilege Club members," says the woman at the
check-in desk.

"I was *told* to come to this lounge," I reply,
standing my ground. I don't volunteer that it was
Chuck who *told* me to try.

After the woman and I repeat ourselves several
times and she figures out that I am not leaving, she
offers me a day pass for $44 and I accept. The big
lounge is nearly empty. A sheik, smoking furiously,
sits in one corner of the lounge while two
international aid workers discuss their assignment a
few chairs away. I eat a cheese sandwich, order a glass
of nondescript white wine, and stare out the window,
waiting to go home.

* * * * *

I learned from my millennial kids, Juliet and Danny,
that there is more than one type of fun.

There is Type I fun, which is truly fun. The short view and the long view feel the same. In other words, it's fun at the time and also when you look back on it. Type II fun is the kind of fun that isn't fun at the time but becomes fun in retrospect. The short view and the long view are different.

My kids say that Type III fun isn't really a thing, but I think it is. The way I look at it, Type III is never fun, neither when you are in the moment nor when you remember it. In fact, you probably try hard to forget Type III fun. The short view and the long view of Types I and III fun are the same.

Type II fun has everything to do with perspective. If you think about it in terms of a landscape, the view from a distance offers lush grassy terraces in the foreground, a blue ribbon of river in the midsection, and white-capped mountains rising to meet the sky. This long view is reassuring for its very distance. It can be very scenic from where you stand.

The short view, however, places you on the edge of the big river as it rushes past. Suddenly, you are not just looking at the landscape, but you are also in it. The same is true of Type II fun: it's great to look back on, full of funny stories, lessons learned, and near misses. But when you are in the thick of it, you probably wouldn't characterize it as a rollicking good time. You don't know at the time if you will skid into the unfortunate "not fun ever" category.

This adventure falls squarely in the category of Type II fun.

The subtitle of this book, "Not every idea is a good idea, but you don't know until you try" may not be your definition of any type of fun, but trying new things does deliver its own payoff. I'm not sorry I said yes to joining Chuck's small expedition to the top of the world and had the guts to go on, even when things didn't turn out like I planned. Remember, they never do.

The willingness to adapt plans and pivot in new directions teaches us to stay light on our feet and keep trying. By giving ourselves permission to try and fail, to make mistakes, we can stretch a little further, step outside of our routine, and get off autopilot.

In the mountains, I had to make decisions in a hot minute about whether to continue or turn back. I guess this is what people mean when they talk about being present. You have to shift your focus to the here-and-now and make decisions based upon the information you have at the time and your gut instincts on how to process it.

You also have to forgive yourself if everything doesn't go as planned. This isn't terribly unlike life itself. You scan the facts as you know them and assign them to a quick checklist of potential pros and cons. Then you weigh that checklist and make a decision. After that comes the hard part—you resolve to follow through, be happy with your choice, and not complain. That pretty much sums up whether you can live in peace with the decisions you make. Or whether you beat yourself up for making a mistake.

When I wrote about walking El Camino de Santiago with Juliet, I talked about the fact that the body knows how to walk and, once you set it in motion, it frees up your mind to think. That made my walk on El Camino filled with reflection and gratitude. In fact, I was overwhelmed with gratitude. Walking the Camino felt like a once-in-a-lifetime opportunity to spend time with my daughter, sharing an adventure that we could laugh about and recount for years. I hoped that we could build a reservoir of goodwill and good stories between us.

Walking 500 miles was not without its physical and emotional challenges, but the scenery was restorative and the community of pilgrims along the way filled it with engaging conversations and friendship. Finally, there was a profound spiritual reward that came from reconnecting to my Catholic faith.

I didn't experience those same rewards on this trip. The constant change of plans required that I spend every moment concentrating on what I was doing and problem-solving about what to do next. That was exhausting. I was lonely, and while you might argue that I was not alone since I was traveling with Ram and Som, I was wrung out by needing to be hypervigilant at every turn. Nobody was there to help me sort out next steps or to talk to about what I should do.

Frequently, I dig into my own soul and ask, how did I change from this trek on the Annapurna Circuit? What did I learn? Should I have bothered?

One of the greatest lessons for me has been that it's okay to make mistakes. If you're shooting for perfection and are afraid of making mistakes, you'll never go anywhere. You'll never do anything. If you do go somewhere, fear may be the only companion you take along.

Elizabeth Gilbert, the *New York Times* best-selling author of *Eat Pray Love*, unmasked perfection by calling it out for the grand lie that is: perfection is not a virtue but "fear in high heels and a mink coat, pretending to be fancy. But it's just terror." This trek was an exercise in not letting my fears ruin everything and turning my mistakes into something bigger than they really were.

I may have put myself to a test that I wasn't quite ready for. But here's the thing: if you wait until you think you're ready, you may never act.

And if you take enough adventures and try enough new things, you are bound to face a sliding scale of success. Even when you carefully plan and mitigate your risks, some experiences will not be what you expect. As I look back at my decades of adventure travel, I realize that the stories I remember most fondly are the ones that didn't go as planned. I think about how adversity shapes us and hardens the ground in front of us, preparing us for our next step.

There is a certain triumph in misadventure. This story would be like thousands of other treks on the Annapurna Circuit if it had not involved a series of unfortunate events that constantly changed my plans, along with poor conditions following a devastating earthquake, and my own obsession with the tragedy on the high pass the year before.

Life gets messy. Sometimes we're afraid. We want everything to go as planned and then we get thrown a curve ball we didn't see coming. So, we take a swing and remind ourselves that it's okay to be afraid. After all, there is no courage without the presence of fear. It's not about the absence of fear, it's about how to manage it. Like Winston Churchill said, "Success is not final; failure is not fatal. It is the courage to continue that counts."

You don't have to book your trip to the Himalayas tomorrow. After reading this, you might think "That's the last thing I'd want to do!" But I hope you will find your own opportunity to disrupt what may be feeling too comfortable and take a risk on yourself. You might find a whole new source of joy and understanding. Maybe that will be a new destination that feeds your wandering soul, a new type of cuisine that spices up your life, or a new subject to learn that nourishes your mind. Maybe you will reawaken your heart by allowing yourself to love again. Or be loved.

The risk of trying something new, whatever that may be, has its own rewards. Even if you have to reach deep to persevere, even if you chalk up the experience to life's lessons and place it in the category of "now I know." Worse than trying and failing is not trying and never knowing. At least for me.

So, go ahead, get out there, and get curious. You don't have to travel to the other side of the world like I did to show up, swallow hard, and be willing to make a mistake. Remember, it's never a mistake to take a risk on yourself.

FIVE YEARS LATER

After Chuck returned to Belfast, he got himself medically checked out. Though asymptomatic, Chuck had been operating for some time with only one out of four main arteries functioning properly. The other three were either nearly or completely clogged. He underwent critical triple bypass surgery to correct the damage and was thankful for a new lease on life when he wrote the following to me:

> "Five years later, at the age of seventy-five, I'm still active, and I'm healthier than I've been in many years. My collie dog, Finn, takes me out walking four to five miles every day on the local hills, rivers, wetlands, and woodlands that surround Belfast. I'm planning a wild camp in the mountains with my son Ben, and the last half of the Camino still awaits. I haven't lost that sense of adventure and, though the Himalayas are probably in the past, there are many other things on my list that I'd like to do. 'Experiences over possessions' is still my mantra.

"I fully understand your observation that dealing with adversity and difficulty can be a positive learning experience for us all. The central and most important revelation for me was that without my experience on the trail, I might never have become aware of my own critical vulnerability. Who knows what might have happened? Being asymptomatic can be very dangerous when there is no warning of any impending collapse. In the end, I'm deeply aware and very grateful that I'm still alive and kicking, especially when others that I've been close to are not.

"I'm not a philosopher, but I do believe that we should try to live our lives as fully and richly every day as we can. Everything is transient. We are all moving through, but there is so much to enjoy and do; it's a privilege that we are here. We have a responsibility to take full advantage of that.

"And so, in the end, even though I didn't manage to go over the Thorung La high pass, and even with the subsequent tribulations, my decision to return to the Annapurna region is one that I do not regret.

"I also think the experience helped me move into a new phase with grace as I come to terms with the limitations and the possibilities that aging inevitably impresses upon us all. Tom Paine was right: adventure is still there to seek out."

* * * * *

Today the Annapurna Circuit itself is a much different place than it was during 2015, the year of destruction. The jeep track now stretches well beyond Chame and, in fact, extends most of the way around the circuit. Trekkers can skip large portions and begin walking anywhere along the route. Perhaps they don't need to trek at all; they can ride nearly the entire way.

While this makes remote areas more accessible, road construction has dramatically diminished the appeal of the experience and authenticity of the route. Trekkers complain about sharing the most dangerous road in the world with jeeps that bear down on them while kicking up dust and dirt. New paths are being bushwhacked away from the road, but blazing a new trail in these inhospitable mountains takes time.

Remote villages are benefiting from an injection of money that increased tourism brings, but ecological challenges jeopardize the long-term sustainability of the route. With more people on the circuit, mountain villages are dealing with more of what humans leave behind, including waste and trash. Mounds of wrappers, plastic water bottles, and other items left behind by visitors can be seen scattered along the trail, creating pollution and an eyesore in a pristine part of the world. Some adventure travelers are no longer rating the Annapurna Circuit as one of the best long-distance treks in the world.

The next phase of the trail is a suitable metaphor for the next phase of my life too. The future is not known. Adventure travel is all about grappling with the unknown, moving forward in the face of uncertainty, and testing your footing only by giving it a try; this uncertainty mixes in the same beaker with that incredible elixir of excitement, challenge, and personal growth for one explosive chemical reaction.

I learned a few nuggets of wisdom about myself at the top of the world, but I'm still looking for answers. I wonder where I should look next.

Made in the USA
Middletown, DE
04 December 2020